Praise for *The Lord Is My Shepherd*

"I rarely read the introduction to a book, much less a prologue. But when asked to review Rob's latest book, I wanted to be responsible and read every page, so I dutifully began with the prologue and introduction. By the time I finished, I was quite surprised by how much of a deeper understanding I had gained about a very familiar psalm. And that paled in comparison to what I received from the rest of the book! Not only do I know Psalm 23 better, but I better know the Lord as my shepherd."

—Dr. Bill Jones, President, Columbia International University

"Robert Morgan has chronicled an insightful and inspirational journey through the Twenty-third Psalm. His personal accounts, meaningful illustrations, and biblical references provide a unique and enriching approach to this well-known psalm. The work gives a fresh, heartfelt interpretation of the text and truths of Psalm 23. He has skillfully shown how Psalm 23 can be applied to our everyday lives. Robert Morgan has given the Christian community a great treasure that I will use often."

—James Flanagan,
President of Luther Rice University and Seminary

"Rob uses Psalm 22, 23, and 24 to show a triad picture of how the Great Shepherd of the sheep wants to take care of our past, present, and future needs. Rob's insight into Psalm 23 is spot on, because of his relationship with the Sovereign Shepherd and his experience both shepherding and sheep-herding. His personal stories will have you gripping your heart, weeping, rejoicing, and ultimately ruminating upon Psalm 23."

—U.S. Army Chaplain (CPT) W. Lee Frye,
442nd Battalion Chaplain, Fort Gordon, GA

Praise for Rob Morgan

"Robert J. Morgan (is) a great writer whose articles have been featured in *Decision Magazine*."

—Franklin Graham

"Rob, you made my day."

—Ruth Bell Graham

"Let me tell you about my friend Robert Morgan. I've got his books all over my nightstand because I just love the way he writes."

—Janet Parshall, nationwide radio host
for the Moody Broadcasting Network

"Rob Morgan has been singly blessed by the Spirit of God with extraordinary ability to exegete the Scriptures with clarity. He has a rare gift for communicating complex ideas in simple language."

—M. A. Henderson,
Executive Director Emeritus of the Gideons International

"Robert Morgan has become a favorite author of our '100 Huntley Street' TV viewers. His poignant illustrations and penetrating scriptural insights are a breath of fresh air to the soul!"

—Ron Mainse, host, "100 Huntley Street,"
and President of Crossroads Christian Communications

"For years Robert Morgan has inspired me with his pastoral insights and heartfelt storytelling."

—Steven James, award-winning author and storyteller

"Rob Morgan has done it again—encouragement on steroids!"

—Dr. Vernon Whaley, Director,
The Center for Worship, Liberty University

"Rob Morgan is a compelling communicator."

—Jim Burns, author, speaker, founder of HomeWord Ministries

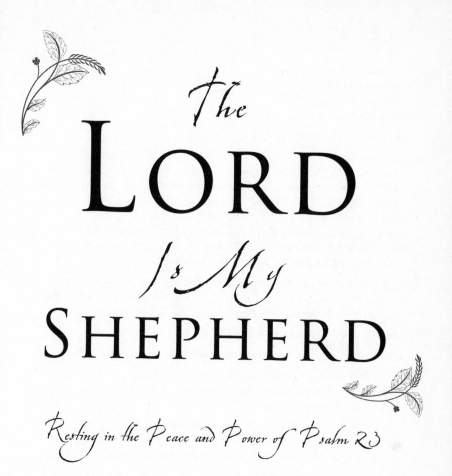

The LORD Is My SHEPHERD

Resting in the Peace and Power of Psalm 23

ROBERT J. MORGAN

Howard Books
A Division of Simon & Schuster, Inc.
New York   Nashville   London   Toronto   Sydney   New Delhi

Howard Books
A Division of Simon & Schuster, Inc.
1230 Avenue of the Americas
New York, NY 10020

First Howard Books hardcover edition February 2013

HOWARD and colophon are trademarks of Simon & Schuster, Inc.

For information about special discounts for bulk purchases,
please contact Simon & Schuster Special Sales at 1-866-506-1949
or business@simonandschuster.com.

The Simon & Schuster Speakers Bureau can bring authors to your live event. For more information or to book an event, contact the Simon & Schuster Speakers Bureau at 1-866-248-3049 or visit our website at www.simonspeakers.com.

Designed by Davina Mock-Maniscalco

Manufactured in the United States of America

10 9 8 7 6 5 4 3 2 1

Library of Congress Cataloging-in-Publication Data
Morgan, Robert J., 1952–
  The Lord is my shepherd : practicing the peace and the power of Psalm 23 / Robert J. Morgan.
    p. cm
1. Bible O.T. Psalms XXIII—Criticism, interpretation, etc. I. Title.
BS145023rd .M67 2013
223'.206—dc23   2012028992

ISBN 978-1-4516-6472-0
ISBN 978-1-4516-6473-7 (ebook)

To
Jude Robert Wu-Jin Rowe

Contents

Prologue

 When my wife and I moved into a new house some years ago—one that had a pasture in the back—our three daughters begged for a horse to ride. We made a counteroffer: we suggested sheep, which seemed smaller, gentler, and more manageable than horses. The girls were none too excited about it until they went to pick out their lambs. But the moment they saw the wooly little things, they were hooked. Furthermore, I was glad for my crew of obliging creatures to regularly mow (and fertilize) the extended backyard. Overnight, our family became shepherds.

We didn't have a large flock, just four or five lambs, and we bottle-fed them till they were old enough to graze on their own. We grew to love those sheep, and they loved us and provided us with a lovely scene out the rear windows every day. We discovered there was nothing more peaceful than getting up in the morning, holding a cup of coffee, and watching our flock of sheep serenely grazing in the dewy meadow.

We're not alone in enjoying the view. In Great Britain, many estates and manors keep sheep purely for ornamental purposes. It's like a page from a children's picture book or a television travel show—cotton balls on green; fat sheep on manicured grounds, grazing, resting, frolicking, baaing, nursing. You can put five to seven ewes and their offspring on the same amount of pasture that will accommodate only one cow and calf, so a small herd of sheep fills out the landscape nicely.

And here's what I've since discovered. With Psalm 23, we can gaze out that evocative window every day. Even if you don't own livestock, it's possible to transport yourself instantly to green pastures, still waters, restored souls, overflowing cups, and righteous pathways.

Now more than ever, we Christians need the peace and power of Psalm 23.

Many of us are far too busy. The stresses of life are wearing us down, little by little, and the noise around us can be an unending cacophony of confusion. Our lives—with all our electronic tethers, emotional entanglements, and financial pressures—are more demanding than ever. We're simply not resting, not managing our clocks and calendars as we'd like, and as a result, we are often anxious and angry, even when we don't realize it. We're pulled in so many directions, as if we were twistable toys in the hands of a toddler.

But consider this: the six verses and about a hundred words of Scripture that make up Psalm 23—the passage that lovingly likens us to sheep—can improve the serenity of our lot every day, because every lot needs a few sheep, and all sheep need a good shepherd.

From the moment it was penned three thousand years ago, the Twenty-third Psalm has been the world's best-known and most-beloved poem. It's been engraved on the hearts of every generation from antiquity to modernity. It's been quoted across the centuries and through the millennia. Its words have blessed millions of sickrooms and thousands of classrooms. It's been quoted in hospitals, jails, homes, and churches; in open-air rallies and underground meetings; in seasons of peace and in times of war. It's been whispered by the bedsides of sleepy children and spoken as the last words of dying convicts. It's the most memorized and memorialized passage in the Bible.

In a hundred words (only fifty-five in the original Hebrew), Psalm 23 sums up all our needs in life and all the abundance of God's grace. It begins with "The Lord," and it ends with "forever." What could be better than that?

"The world could afford to spare many a magnificent library better than it could dispense with this little psalm of six verses," observed William Evans, a writer of yesteryear.[1]

Author Frederick B. Meyer called this small chapter "a microcosm of God's grace." Just as the whole sun is reflected in a single drop of dew, so we see all the grace and the whole gospel of God reflected in Psalm 23.[2]

I grew up near Roan Mountain, on the Tennessee–North Carolina border. The Roan highlands are home to the largest natural rhododendron garden in the world and the longest stretch of grassy balds in the Appalachian Mountains. These treeless, grassy areas boast stunning panoramic views.

Jon and Regina Buck are friends of mine in Roan Mountain.

Jon is my barber. When I told them I was writing a book about the Twenty-third Psalm, Regina told me her story. She and Jon had long prayed for a child, but they waited several years before a baby came along. When little Jace did arrive, he came with a very serious heart defect requiring multiple surgeries. During the times of her greatest stress and fear, Regina told me, she would drive up to the grassy balds at the top of Roan Mountain and lie down in those rich alpine meadows, gazing up at the blue sky. There her nerves would relax and her spirits revive.

"Resting in Psalm Twenty-three is exactly like that," she said. "Lying down in God's green pastures is no less real than lying in the grass at the top of the Roan. There is complete silence. No traffic, no talking, no blaring speakers or animal noises. The grass blows in beautiful waves as the wind shifts. The ground is soft, and the view incredible in every direction. I understand the peace and strength of the creation that God has bestowed on us."[3]

Imagine. Resting in the Shepherd's psalm can be as real as lying down on the vast grassy balds at the highest elevations of the Appalachian Trail. It's a lofty place, a quiet spot, and a passage of great peace and power. We can get there without a plane ticket or road map. The trip is as short as reaching for our Bibles or quoting a verse by heart. It's never further than a moment or a memory.

Years ago, Saturday newspapers routinely carried the sermon topics for the next day in the leading pulpits in town. In Norfolk, Virginia, Reverend R. I. Williams of Fairmont Park Methodist Church picked up the phone and called the local paper to give them his sermon topic.

"The Lord is my Shepherd," he said. The person on the other end said, "Is that all?" Reverend Williams replied, "That's enough." The next day the church page carried his sermon topic as "The Lord Is My Shepherd—That's Enough!"[4]

When the Lord is our Shepherd, that *is* enough. *He* is enough. Enough to meet our needs, calm our nerves, clear our vision, restore our souls, ensure our future, and bless our day.

So take a moment, open the windows, read aloud these timeless words, and practice for yourself the peace and the power of Psalm 23 and its all-sufficient Shepherd.

> *The Lord is my shepherd; I shall not want.*
> *He makes me to lie down in green pastures;*
> *He leads me beside the still waters.*
> *He restores my soul;*
> *He leads me in the paths of righteousness for His name's sake.*
> *Yea, though I walk through the valley of the shadow of death,*
> *I will fear no evil;*
> *For You are with me; Your rod and Your staff, they comfort me.*
> *You prepare a table before me in the presence of my enemies;*
> *You anoint my head with oil; my cup runs over.*
> *Surely goodness and mercy shall follow me all the days of my life.*
> *And I will dwell in the house of the Lord forever.*

Introduction

$\mathcal{M}$aurice Pink, ninety, lives quietly with his wife in a little house in Ipswich, England, about two hours northwest of London. He's a British World War II vet who, during the conflict, was ditched in the open sea on two different occasions when Japanese forces sunk the ships on which he served. Talking with me on a recent Sunday afternoon, Maurice described his "first dunking," as he put it. He was a nineteen-year-old sailor aboard the battle cruiser HMS *Repulse* when five torpedoes struck on December 10, 1941. This was the "British Pearl Harbor." Only three days after the attack on American Naval Forces in Hawaii, the Japanese launched a series of raids on British ships in Malaya. More than eight hundred British sailors perished in the attacks. Maurice's ship, the HMS *Repulse*, sank in seven minutes.

Maurice, who played the cornet with the Royal Marine Band, was in the transmitting station of the *Repulse*, three decks down, talking on the phone. The explosion from the torpedoes threw him across the room and into the bulkhead. The lights went off;

he was trapped. Debris from the explosion blocked the exits and stairways, and there appeared no escape. The ship was sinking fast, and as Maurice struggled to find a way out, he heard the captain's voice over the speakers: "All hands on deck. Prepare to abandon ship. God be with you."

Maurice felt water filling the room and rising up his legs. At once, another sailor, a young midshipman, turned on a flashlight and shouted for Maurice to follow. He knew of a private ladder that led up to the captain's day cabin. They clambered up ladders and through passages, finding to their relief the hatches unlocked.

Arriving at the edge of the deck, Maurice stripped off his clothes and jumped into the lukewarm waters of the South China Sea. He had no life vest, and the area was infested with sharks. Maurice told me he was naked ("not a stitch," he said) and disoriented, unsure which way to swim. If he got too close to the sinking ship, he'd be pulled under by its vortex as it went down. If he got beyond the oil-slicked waters, the sharks would get him. He began to panic.

At that moment, the long-ago memorized words of Psalm 23 came to his mind. As he treaded water, trying to hold on and hold out, he began quoting those words to himself over and over. And the words of Psalm 23 buoyed him up. They were better than a life vest. They kept him unsinkable until the British destroyer HMS *Electra* rescued him more than an hour later.

"Would you like me to read what I've written about my experience?" he asked. I quickly replied in the affirmative, and this is what he read from his penciled notes on a treasured piece of paper:

There are times in your life when things don't go right and you feel all alone. That happened to me on December 10, 1941, when I was on the battle cruiser HMS *Repulse* with the nearby HMS *Prince of Wales*. We were attacked by the Japanese Air Force, which resulted in both ships being sunk. I found myself alone in the water not able to see anyone else. It was then that the Twenty-third Psalm came into my head and I realized I was not alone. I had a Shepherd. The Lord was my Shepherd; I did not need to want. I was not in green pastures but in oily waters; but He restored my soul. Even though I was walking in the shadow of death, I was to fear no evil, for He was with me.

The rod and staff did not ring a bell with me until voices above me were shouting. Looking up, there was a big destroyer alongside me, HMS *Electra*, with nets over the side, which allowed me to climb up to safety. That was my rod and staff. I didn't have a table set before me, but I did get a cup of the ship's kye (or cocoa).

Since that day, goodness and mercy have followed me all the days of my life; and when I think back to that day, I wonder what would have happened if I had died. There again, the psalm had the answer: I would dwell in the house of the Lord forever.

Thank you, Lord, for being my Shepherd and for the Twenty-third Psalm.[1]

God's Triad of Truth

I'm a firm believer that Psalm 23 can keep our heads above water when our ship is going down. That's why it's important to memorize it, visualize it, study it, pray it, sing it, and to understand that it's located in the very center of the Bible, in the heart of Scripture. It's even notable that this chapter is flanked between Psalms 22 and 24.

The Lord didn't assemble His Word haphazardly. Though written over a period of nearly one thousand five hundred years by more than forty authors on three continents and in three languages, the Bible is the most brilliantly compiled book in the world. Every part fits the next like an interlocking puzzle. The more I study Scripture—and I've been doing so for about fifty years—the more I'm awed by its balance and beauty, and by the blueprint that connects each chapter and book with the whole.

This is particularly true of the book of Psalms. There are 150 psalms, but as we study each one, it's helpful to notice the one preceding it and the one following it. Often there are enriching links. For example, Psalm 23 is not merely floating around in Scripture like a cloud. Its secure location, between Psalm 22 and Psalm 24, is not by accident. It's actually a part of a trilogy of Messianic Psalms about the yet-to-come Savior. So the first step in understanding Psalm 23 is knowing its setting and understanding its location within the trio of Psalms 22 through 24. These three chapters present the whole story of the Gospel of God's grace and answer our three greatest questions: What about my past? My present? My future? Therein lay all our worries, for every problem is either behind us, around us, or before us.

Tension comes in three tenses. We worry about the mistakes and misfortunes of yesterday or yesteryear; we're anxious about today with its trials and troubles; and we are apprehensive about the future, which is as uncertain as the wind.

Hence Psalm 22, Psalm 23, and Psalm 24—God's triad of truth to deal with life, whatever tense we're in.

Psalm 22 is one of the most momentous Messianic chapters in the Old Testament. Penned a thousand years before Calvary, Psalm 22 gives us the very words Jesus would later speak from the cross. The conversations of His persecutors are also prequoted. Psalm 22 predicts the traumas Christ would suffer during His crucifixion, including His stripping, piercing, thirst, exposure, insults, humiliation, and death. It's as if the psalmist were standing at the foot of the cross painting the scene like at artist, though the event was still a millennium away. It's as if the psalmist were describing the action as a journalist.

Psalm 22 begins: "My God, My God, why have You forsaken Me?" Because Jesus was forsaken, we are forgiven. Because He was beaten, we are healed. Because He was thirsty, we're awash in the water of life. Because He died, we have an eternal home. No matter how deep our regrets, how searing our conscience, how messy our past, we start each day with a clean slate. All our failures are washed away in His blood. Psalm 22 ends with the declaration: "They will come and declare His righteousness to a people who will be born, that He has done this."

Finishing the crucifixion scene in Psalm 22, the next line in our Bibles reads: "Psalm 23." Suddenly we're in the care of the risen Christ, the Good Shepherd who laid down His life for His sheep and who now longs to tend to our present needs. Notice that almost all the verbs in the Twenty-third Psalm are in the present tense. This is a psalm for today: He makes me, He leads me, He restores, He guides, He is with me, He comforts me, He prepares a table for me, He anoints; my cup overflows. His shepherding ministries are for today.

I like what John Stevenson said about this psalm nearly 150 years ago: "The Twenty-third Psalm commends itself to the heart of the believer by its own internal excellence. Natural in its structure, simple and perspicuous in its language, and elegant and attractive in its imagery, it breathes forth sentiments of confidence towards God, of gratitude and of joy. There is a depth of meaning in every sentence—a rich variety of experience in every verse—and a fullness of joy from its commencement to its conclusion, which comprehends all that is needed in life and in death, in time and throughout eternity."[2]

Psalm 23 takes care of today.

As we continue reading our trilogy of psalms, our eyes fall on the next line of biblical text: Psalm 24 and its opening declaration: "The earth is the Lord's, and all its fullness." As we read the ten verses of Psalm 24, we're taken to the glorious city of our soon-coming king. "Lift up your heads, O you gates! And be lifted up, you everlasting doors! And the King of Glory shall come in."

Psalm 24 is a description of the joy of the enthronement of

Jesus Christ, the King of Glory, the everlasting Lord of hosts. It reminds us that He provides everlasting life and joy for His children. He Himself is the resurrection and the life, and because He lives, we shall live also. One day soon, we will see Him in all His glory. One day soon, He'll come for us, or we'll go to Him. All our enemies are defeated. All our problems are temporary. All our blessings are eternal. While everything about this world is transient, everything about the New Heavens and the New Earth is transcendent.

Psalm 24 is a glorious three-part poem that focuses on the greatness of the Creator (v. 1–2), the privilege of coming into His presence in worship (v. 3–6), and the nearing day when the King will come to claim His Kingdom (v. 7–10). All our apprehensions will be lost in celebration, and all our sorrows will be drowned out by music accompanying the King of Glory.

These three psalms are a threefold picture of the ministry that flows from the Messiah's heart into our needs, whether past, present, or future. He is the same yesterday, today, and forever. The savior's cross takes care of yesterday. The shepherd's crook takes care of today. The sovereign's crown takes care of tomorrow.

Psalm 22 takes us to Mount Calvary. Psalm 24 centers around Mount Zion. Between them—where we are living now—is the lovely valley of Psalm 23 with its the gentle pastures, sloping meadows, and dramatic canyons.

As an old divine once said: "To have Jehovah for a Shepherd—to feel no want—to enjoy rest and peace, restoration and guidance—and to fear no evil in the last hour of nature's extremity—to be the guest of God, to have a table provided—

honor conferred—abundance supplied—goodness and mercy following us through life—and the house of the Lord as our dwelling place forever, are blessings so transcendent and desirable, that as we read this Psalm we almost instinctively turn it into a prayer: 'Lord, be Thou my Shepherd.'"[3]

Our Shepherd holds us safely, and He alone can take care of our past, our present, and our future, whether in green pastures or oily waters, whether lying on our backs in a highland meadow or treading water in the open sea.

Part 1

THE LORD IS MY SHEPHERD

The Twenty-third Psalm is the greatest poem
ever penned in any language. It reigns supreme in circles
of highest culture and in the humble homes of the lowly.
It sounds all the chords of human experience.

—Dr. Robert C. McQuilkin[1]

1

"The Lord Is . . ."

PSALM 23:1

$\mathcal{M}$y father, John I. Morgan, was the owner of Sunset Orchard on the Tennessee and North Carolina border and a high school professor specializing in vocational agriculture, so I grew up around gardens, orchards, and livestock—especially ponies, horses, and burros. But we never raised sheep, so when Katrina and I later purchased our small flock, we hardly knew what we were doing. A helpful friend told us about a classic book on shepherding entitled *Raising Sheep the Modern Way*. Now published as an updated version under the title *Storey's Guide to Raising Sheep*, this book proved a valuable resource not only for raising sheep but also for understanding the Twenty-third Psalm.

The authors, Paula Simmons and Carol Ekarius, begin the book saying, "When you decide to get sheep, it helps if you understand their behavior—in other words, what makes them tick. The more you understand about their behavior, the easier it will be for you to spot problems (for example, is that ewe in the corner sick or is she about to lamb?). Understanding behavior also makes handling animals much easier, on both you and them."

The authors describe a healthy flock this way: "Sheep that are behaving normally are content and alert. They have good appetites and bright eyes. They are gregarious animals, which contributes to their flocking nature. Youngsters, like those of other species, love to play and roughhouse. Groups of lambs will run, romp, and climb for hours when they are healthy and happy. Then they'll fall asleep so deeply that you may think they're dead."[2]

King David could have written those words three thousand years ago. He understood the contrast between healthy sheep and distressed ones, and he knew the difference was often determined by the quality of shepherding and the nature of the shepherd. Sheep, shepherds, lambs, and flocks are mentioned nearly seven hundred times in the Bible (698 times to be exact, in 563 verses in the New King James Version). The sheep is the first animal mentioned by name in the Bible (Genesis 4:2, Amplified Bible).

Roy Gustafson, dean of tour guides to Israel who conducted more than 150 trips to Bible lands before his death in 2002, once related a story of a missionary in the mountains of Turkey who gathered a group of shepherds to read the Bible to them. It was a cold night, and as they sat around a fire, the missionary read from the tenth chapter of John about the good shepherd, the thief, the hireling, the sheep, and the door to the sheepfold.

"Oh, sir, is that in the Gospel?" asked one of the shepherds in surprise.

"Yes," said the missionary, "that is the Gospel of Jesus Christ."

"Oh," said the shepherd, the glow of the fire lighting his eyes, "I didn't know before that the Bible was a sheep book."[3]

Well, it is. The Bible is populated by millions of sheep. On one occasion, the Jews seized 650,000 sheep from the Midianites. The Assyrian king Sennacherib took 800,000 from his enemy's lands. King Ahab demanded 100,000 rams as tribute from the king of Moab. At the dedication of the Temple in Jerusalem, King Solomon offered 120,000 sheep as sacrifices, and we're told that 300,000 sacrificial animals were offered annually in Jerusalem.[4]

Many of the biblical heroes were shepherds, and chief among them was David—musician, herdsman, warrior king, and intrepid giant killer. Some of the most vivid shepherding material comes from his life and writings. Our mind's eye can readily see this lad in his youth, clad in weathered leather and armed with his staff. His slingshot and shepherd's pouch hang on his belt; he has lute and lyre at hand.

Looking at him in the distance, we're impressed with his expressive face, his reddish hair, his muscular yet lithe frame. There he is, leaning against a boulder, keeping a sharp eye on his flocks, calling his sheep by name, composing songs on the fly, and enjoying life to the fullest. He weathers the elements with ruggedness, maintains his flocks with warmhearted discipline, and eliminates predators with coldblooded efficiency.

We first meet David in the sixteenth chapter of 1 Samuel, when the prophet Samuel arrived in Bethlehem looking for young men with royal potential. A local farmer named Jesse had a houseful of sons who seemed to fit the bill, and he trotted out his boys for inspection. Samuel was impressed with these young men, but the Lord wasn't. Seeing the eldest, Eliab, Samuel thought to himself, "Surely the Lord's anointed is before Him." But the Lord said to Samuel, "Do not look at his appearance or at his physical stature . . . for the Lord does not see as a man sees; for man looks at the outward appearance, but the Lord looks at the heart." That's sage advice for us in today's age of glitz and glamour, where people have become "brands" and celebrities are made to appear as though they have as much depth as rain on a sidewalk.

After the remainder of Jesse's sons had passed before Samuel and been rejected, the aged prophet asked, "Are all the young men here?"

"There remains yet the youngest," Jesse said, "and there he is, keeping the sheep."

The boy was summoned. He was "ruddy, with bright eyes, and good looking." But there was a depth to him, acquired amid the rocky fields of Judea from the solitude of shepherding. He had a good and God-fearing heart. Samuel's wrinkled hand reached for his flask of oil. Motioning for the boy to kneel, the old prophet anointed the young shepherd to be the future king of Israel, and the Spirit of the Lord came on David from that day (1 Samuel 16:1–13).

This was the boy who wrote Psalm 23. This was the man after God's own heart. The profession of shepherding became a classroom for the crown. It was God's apprenticeship for kingship. In loving his sheep, David learned to care for his people. While protecting his flock, David was preparing to guard his nation. As he led his animals from pasture to pasture, he acquired the skills of leading men and guiding armies. No experiences were lost, as the fields of Bethlehem became a laboratory for leadership.

The same, of course, is true for us. Wherever we are today and whatever we're doing, it's simply preparation for future service. No experiences should be wasted, and a day is never lost if a lesson is learned. We all have goals and aspirations, but our primary job isn't to envision great things in the future but to tackle today's work with enthusiasm. This is true whatever our age. Our best days are always ahead of us, and our present experiences are preparing us for greater work in the future, whether on earth or in heaven. David cared for his flocks as if there were no tomorrow. In the process, God was preparing him for tomorrow's greatness.

Nor did David ever forget the spiritual lessons he learned during his solitary epochs in those distant pastures and lonely hillsides. In being a shepherd, he learned to think of himself as a sheep, trusting the Lord to do for him what he was doing for his flocks. He pondered the parallel long and hard, and he later summed it all up in the most reassuring words ever written: *"The Lord Is my Shepherd."*

The Lord . . .

The actual word David used in Psalm 23:1 is *Yahweh*, the proper and the personal name of God as He made Himself known to the people of Israel. As far as we can determine, it comes from the Hebrew word meaning "to be" or "I am." The Bible's primary text on this subject is Exodus 3, when God had earlier appeared to another shepherd—Moses—in the burning bush. When Moses asked God for His name, the answer came back: "I AM WHO I AM."

The Hebrew consonants for "I AM" serve as the basis for the name *Yahweh*. To the Hebrews, this name was too sacred to speak, so they substituted the term *Adonai,* which means "The Lord." Most English translations have followed suit by printing the word Lord in small caps. As German theologians of an earlier century tried to sort out the vowels and consonants, they translated the Hebrew word as *Jehovah.* Many of the older books on Psalm 23 use the term *Jehovah-Roi,* which means "The Lord—my Shepherd!"

More recently, scholars have suggested the pronunciation *Yahweh* (YAH-way) is closer to the original.[5] But whether you say *Lord, Jehovah, Adonai,* or *Yahweh,* the meaning seems to touch on this idea: "I Am Who I Am—God almighty, unchanging and unchangeable. I Am self-sustaining, self-existent—the Creator, not the created. I Was, and I Am, and I Will Be—from everlasting to everlasting, First and Last, Beginning and End, Alpha and Omega."

This is tremendous to think about, for what often is missing from our lives is the contemplation of God. We spend hours contemplating finances or projects or problems or family matters. We obsess over many stressful things, and then, to forget about them, we pursue an array of diversions unmatched in history. Many of us have become afraid of a quiet mind. Yet when we learn to practice consciously the presence of God, meditating on His Word and contemplating His attributes, it has a remarkable effect on our brains and thereby on our personalities.

When we look up into a cloudy sky, as David often did from his hilltop perch, seeing bare tree limbs gnarled against a gray sky, it reveals the creative genius of He who planted the trees and fashioned the clouds. When we read a verse of Scripture such as Psalm 23:1 and look at it word for word, we are changed as we reflect on it. We memorize it. We roll its words around in our minds like stones in a tumbler. We ponder the infinities of the God who is, who has presently spoken to us, who has eternally given us His Word. Because God is God, our minds are swallowed up in His immensity.

In a recent sermon, I put it this way: I live in a bend of the Cumberland River, which snakes through Tennessee and Kentucky for seven hundred miles before dumping its waters into the Ohio River. Imagine walking with me to the end of my street, standing on the riverbank, and trying to squeeze those billions of rolling gallons into a single medicine dropper pulled from my pocket. That would be easier than absorbing all the knowledge of the Almighty. Our minds simply can't fathom infinitude. Contemplating the limitless glories of the Creator leaves us boggled and overwhelmed. But the truth is this: we are blessed in being boggled, and undergirded by being overwhelmed.

Properly thinking about *Yahweh* expands our minds. It humbles our hearts, balances our thoughts, clarifies our perspectives, reassures our spirits, and strengthens our souls. As we think rightly about God, everything else assumes proper proportions.

He is true, noble, just, pure, lovely, admirable, excellent, and praiseworthy; the Bible tells us to "meditate on these things," as advised by the apostle Paul in Philippians 4:8. Memorizing chapters such as Psalm 23 and Philippians 4, training ourselves to mull over those passages as we get up, as we go to bed, as we drive to work, as we hike the trails—that's a practice that transfigures and transforms us.

We are who we are because He Is Who He Is. All other life in the universe is derived. Whether a tree or a plant, a bird or an animal, a person or an angel—we have a beginning. We're created, hence creatures. But He derived His life from no one and from nowhere. He alone is the Creator. The Bible says, "Now to the King eternal, immortal, invisible, to God who alone is wise, be honor and glory forever and ever. Amen" (1 Timothy 1:17). Any lesser Lord couldn't meet our needs.

We need a God of justice, for a universe without moral foundations is a catastrophe. We need a God of love, for we're all sinners. We need an omnipotent God, because it's critical for all things to work together for good. We need an omnipresent God, for even one moment without Him is disastrous. We need an omniscient God, because our wisdom is deficient and defective. We need a God of resurrection, for we long for permanent reunions. We need a God who is eternal, for we have eternity in our hearts. We need exactly the kind of God the Bible describes as our Shepherd—*Jehovah-Roi. Adonai.*

The title *Adonai* later became the Greek God-word employed by New Testament writers to describe the divine nature of Jesus Christ. That's why the apostle Paul, for example, frequently spoke of "*God* the Father and the *Lord* Jesus Christ." As the New Testament writers alluded to the Trinity, they tended to refer to the Father as *God* (*Theos*) and the Son as *Lord* (*Adonai*). Both are Old Testament God-words. Both names imply deity or

Godness, yet they allow a distinction between the members of the Godhead.

In the original language of the New Testament, Jesus Christ is *Adonai Yeshua*—the Lord Jesus. *Adonai* (Lord) is a positional title. *Yeshua* is a personal name meaning "The Lord Saves." The Hebrew version of *Yeshua* is *Joshua*. In English, it's *Jesus*.

By His own testimony, *Adonai Yeshua* stepped into the Shepherd's role described in Psalm 23 and claimed it for Himself. He wrapped Himself in the verses of Psalm 23 the way an ancient shepherd would put on his cloak. Jesus became Psalm 23 personified. As He explained in the Gospel of John, "The thief does not come except to steal, and to kill, and to destroy. I have come that they may have life, and that they may have it more abundantly. I am the good shepherd. The good shepherd gives His life for the sheep" (John 10:10–11).

So we say with full biblical accuracy *Yeshua is my shepherd.* The book of Hebrews calls Jesus "that great shepherd of the sheep" (Hebrews 13:20), and Peter told his readers, "For you were like sheep going astray, but have now returned to the Shepherd and Overseer of your souls" (1 Peter 2:25). He was referring to the Lord Jesus who is both God and man, both divine and human, both infinite and intimate. Revelation 7:17 says about Jesus: "The Lamb who is in the midst of the throne will shepherd them."

Many times, I've found indescribable comfort in that mystery. Though He has neither beginning of days nor end of life, the Lord Jesus cares about all our mornings and evenings. Though He created everything and was created by no one, He intricately crafted us in our mothers' wombs. Though He fashioned Orion with its bright stars and the Big Dipper with its angular points, His tenderness covers our wildest fears and mildest woes. His thunder rolls through the night, yet His Word whispers in our ears. He who counts the stars also heals the brokenhearted and lifts up the humble. He fills the universe, yet He is always near His children and His flock.

. . . *Is* . . .

Let's go on to the next word, *is*: "*The Lord is.*" Though a tiny word—one syllable, two letters—*is* has a double meaning with enormous significance.

First, the word *is* connotes existence. If something *is,* it exists. That's why we call it a "being verb." God exists. He is. The Lord is. This is the tiny word that confounds atheists. I've been interested in the proliferation of atheistic billboards and bus signs sprouting up like weeds all over the world. They often say something like "Millions Are Good Without God." Or "In the Beginning Man Created God." Or "There's Probably No God." I saw a picture of one atheistic billboard during the Christmas season bearing the words "Heathen's Greetings!" It doesn't take a lot of intelligence to slap drivel on the sides of buses or buildings.

As I'm writing this book, a report surfaced about a church in Johannesburg, South Africa, that posted an opposing billboard. It showed a young man deep in thought but with an empty head. Accompanying the image was a quotation from the British poet Francis Thompson, who said, "An atheist is a man who believes himself to be an accident." City officials promptly deemed the billboard offensive to atheists and had it pulled down.

Recently the headlines from London told of a famous professor, Richard Dawkins, who surprised his fellow atheists by confessing that he should probably call himself an agnostic since he can't prove that God doesn't exist. As the author of *The God Delusion* and a champion of Darwinist evolution, his statement stunned the audience where he was speaking and sent shock waves through atheistic circles.[6]

I believe that Christians, on the other hand, can hold their theism with intellectual credibility based on clear logic, sound reasoning, and compelling evidence. We not only believe in God, but we also believe that by His very nature He must be personal. We have so many sheeplike qualities built into us that we can truly think of the Creator as our Lord and Shepherd. No campaign by radical atheists can shake the impregnability of that tiny word *is*. It denotes existence, even as the Bible opens with the words: *In the beginning God . . .*

There's a second implication of this verb. Those two letters—*is*—indicate not only *existence* but also *immediacy*. The present tense. The sentence does not say The Lord *was* my Shepherd, or He *will be* my Shepherd. He *is* my Shepherd, presently. Jesus, though timeless and eternal, is now and He is accessible, a God of the moment, a God of every moment.

The word *is* isn't a promise, for a promise is a statement that declares what God is *going to do* in the future. The Bible is full of precious promises. In a wide assortment of verses, the Lord tells us: "I will do this; I will do that," and the verbs are typically in future tense. The promises of God are His guarantees amid life's uncertainties.

But Psalm 23:1 is written in the present tense; it's a verb that doesn't await fulfillment. Rather than a prediction, it's a fact. It implies something God is doing presently. It's not a promise to claim, but a reality to experience. Our Lord is a Shepherd whose presence is instant, immediate, and accessible every day, every hour, every moment. Read the following Bible verses and notice the italicized verbs *is* and *are* that follow the great nouns that refer to our Lord:

- "Surely the Lord *is* in this place, and I did not know it."—Genesis 28:16

- "The Lord *is* my strength and my song."—Exodus 15:2

- "The eternal God *is* your refuge, and underneath *are* the everlasting arms."—Deuteronomy 33:27

- "The Lord *is* my light and my salvation; whom shall I fear? The Lord *is* the strength of my life; of whom shall I be afraid?"—Psalm 27:1

- "God *is* our refuge and strength, a very present help in trouble."—Psalm 46:1

- "The Lord *is* in His holy temple."—Habakkuk 2:19

- "God *is* faithful"—1 Corinthians 1:9

- "God *is* stronger"—1 Corinthians 1:25

- "God *is* holy"—1 Corinthians 3:17

- "God *is* for us,"—Romans 8:31

- "God *is* able"—2 Corinthians 9:8

- "Before Abraham was, *I AM*."—John 8:58

- "*I am* the Bread of life . . . *I am* the light of the world . . .
  I am the door . . . *I am* the resurrection and the life . . .
  I am the good shepherd,"—John 6:35, 8:12, 10:9,
  11:25, 10:11[7]

Some years ago when I went through a rough patch and couldn't rest, I found I could fall asleep on the couch by wrapping myself in a blanket and continuously repeating in my mind Psalm 23 with its opening declaration: "The Lord . . . The Lord is . . . The Lord is my . . . The Lord is my Shepherd . . ." This chapter had a calming power I found nowhere else. It was a soul soother, a mental ointment. Mulling over every word was like finding another life preserver.

Many other people share a similar testimony. Recently, I met a friend who's recovering from open-heart surgery. There were complications, and he had a horrendous time. "While I was lying there in intensive care," he said, "I just kept quoting the Twenty-third Psalm to myself over and over. It's what got me through."

Following the devastating 2010 earthquake in Haiti, I read about a woman buried beneath the rubble. It took several days for rescuers to reach her. By continuously quoting the Twenty-third Psalm, she survived and was saved.

I heard of another man who went through a day of such incredible stress and anxiety that, according to his later testimony, he quoted the Twenty-third Psalm a hundred times between sunup to sundown.

Psalm 23:1 is the world's most powerful opening for history's most precious poem: *The Lord is* . . . He is Yahweh God. He is Yeshua Jesus. He is here, and He is here now for you and me.

The Lord is our shepherd!

The Twenty-third Psalm is the best-known chapter
in the Bible—and the least understood.
It is the best-loved chapter in the Bible—
and the least believed.

—Dr. Robert C. McQuilkin[1]

2

"My"

PSALM 23:1

According to an old story, two hikers in the Welsh mountains came upon a young man keeping his sheep. The fellow's rustic profession charmed the travelers, and they talked with him at length about shepherding. The conversation turned to the Twenty-third Psalm.

"Think of the five fingers of your left hand," one of the men told the boy. "Let each finger stand for a word. You can meditate on Psalm 23:1 by grasping each finger, one at a time, with your right hand."

Showing him how to do it, the man gripped his thumb and said, "That stands for *The*. That's an emphatic beginning. Next, your index finger stands for the word *Lord*." Grasping his index finger, the man told the boy to ponder the goodness and grace of the Lord Jesus, who loved him.

Touching his longest finger, the man said, "This finger stands for the word *is*. The Lord is alive and here with you right now, in the present tense. And the fourth finger stands for the fourth word in the verse: *my*. A wedding ring on the fourth finger, after all, reminds us of the personal and exclusive relationship we have with the one we love. And the little finger—the pinky—stands for *shepherd*. When you come to the end of your hand, or to the end of any task, even to the end of life, you find the Shepherd still there, abiding with you always."

The boy, who seldom encountered travelers in the Welsh highlands, enjoyed the conversation very much and drank in every word.

The following year the men returned on another hiking trip, and this time they stopped at a small wayfaring house for a cup of tea. On the table was a picture of the very boy they had met a year before. They asked about him, and the woman put down her cup, composed herself, and said, "Yes, that was my son. He died last winter in a storm. He fell down a cliff and lay there a long time. Only later did we find him."

In the ensuing stillness she added, "There was something strange about it, though, which we've never understood. When we found his body, his right hand was grasping the fourth finger of his left hand."

"Ah," said one of the men with a soft smile, "we can explain that." They told the mother what had happened the previous year. In gripping his finger, the boy was reminding himself that the Lord was *his* Shepherd, even at life's end. It was a comfort in his hour of need, and an unspeakable gift to his mother to hear the story.[2]

Martin Luther once said that the heart of Christianity is seen in its personal pronouns, and Psalm 23 is full of them. Try this exercise. Read Psalm 23 aloud, giving an emphasis to every circled word—each a personal pronoun. Notice all the *He*s and *Me*s.

> The Lord is (my) shepherd; (I) shall not want.
> (He) makes (me) to lie down in green pastures;
> (He) leads (me) beside the still waters.
> (He) restores (my) soul;
> (He) leads (me) in the paths of righteousness for (His) name's sake.
> Yea, though (I) walk through the valley of the shadow of death,
> (I) will fear no evil;
> For (You) are with (me); (Your) rod and (Your) staff, (they) comfort (me.)
> (You) prepare a table before (me) in the presence of (my) enemies;
> (You) anoint (my) head with oil; (my) cup runs over.
> Surely goodness and mercy shall follow (me)
> all the days of (my) life.
> And (I) will dwell in the house of the Lord forever.

All told, there are twenty-eight personal pronouns in these six verses—about 25 percent of the entire text! No wonder William Evans, a writer of a hundred years ago, observed that the Twenty-third Psalm is so *universal* because it was so *individual*.[3]

That little word *my* makes Psalm 23 as personal as our own skin and bones. When we say, "The Lord is *my* Shepherd," we're really saying, "I am His sheep. He owns me, and I'm under His management and care. I have a personal relationship with the God of the universe, a friendship that does for me everything ancient shepherds continually did for their flocks, and more."

The word *shepherd* is a contraction of the term *sheep herder*.

When I entered the ministry as a young pastor in rural East Tennessee, I decided to invest some time studying every passage about sheep and shepherding in the Bible. The reason? I learned that the word *pastor* means "shepherd." It's related to the word *pasture*. Pastors are those who lead their flocks into the nourishment of God's Word. How long it took to track down all the biblical references to sheep, I can't remember. That was in the 1970s before the availability of computers or Bible-related software. It was a matter of tracking down words in a concordance and turning to each passage by hand. But what I discovered has shaped my pastoral work for over three decades.

Biblical shepherds, I learned, could categorize their duties into six divisions: (1) seeking lost and straying livestock (soulwinning and evangelism); (2) feeding the sheep (teaching and preaching); (3) guiding the flocks (leadership); (4) tending the sheep (visiting, counseling, and pastoral care); (5) protecting the herds from predators (ethics, vigilance, doctrinal purity); and, most important, (6) loving their flocks.

The last item is key. I was amazed to discover that in Hebrew, the word for *friend* is derived from the Hebrew term for *shepherd*. In biblical times, it wasn't dogs that were man's best friends, but sheep. They bonded with their shepherds and the shepherds with them.

In his delightful book on the Holy Land, Roy Gustafson told of touring a little oasis, Al Azraq, some fifty-five miles east of Amman, Jordan. On the way back, his group met a shepherd with about one hundred twenty-five sheep. All the tourists reached for their cameras, and as they were snapping and chatting, one of the tour members asked the shepherd, "Do your sheep have names?"

The shepherd instantly turned around and started pointing to each sheep in the flock and telling its name. Gustafson couldn't help recalling what Jesus had said about the Good Shepherd in John 10:3, "He calls His own sheep by name and leads them out." And the Bible tells us that our names are written in the "Lamb's Book of Life."

Perhaps this was the passage that prompted Tommy Walker to write this little chorus: "He knows my name. / He knows my every thought. / He sees each tear that falls / and He hears me when I call."[4]

Charles Spurgeon once observed, "There cannot be a flock without a shepherd; neither is there a shepherd truly without a flock. The two must go together . . . We are Christ's sheep. To belong to a king carries some measure of distinction. We are the sheep of the imperial pastures."[5]

The prophet Isaiah summed it up when he said the Lord "tends His flock like a shepherd; He gathers the lambs in His arms and carries them close to His heart; He gently leads those that have young" (Isaiah 40:11, NIV 84).

The Ninety and Nine

The language of shepherding affection is seen everywhere in Scripture, and it's the greatest single emphasis the Bible offers on this subject. The prophet Ezekiel bemoaned the shepherds in his day who didn't care for their flocks, insisting that the coming Messiah would care for His flock with undying faithfulness. "You are my flock, the sheep of My pasture. You are My people, and I am your God" (Ezekiel 34:31, NLT).

Likewise in Mark 6:34, Jesus was moved with compassion for the multitudes for "they were like sheep not having a shepherd. So He began to teach them many things."

In Luke 15, Jesus told of the ragged-weary shepherd who, while counting his sheep at the end of the day, realized one had strayed off into the "mountains wild and bare . . . away from the tender shepherd's care." Leaving the ninety and nine in the fold, the man returned to the hills calling for his lost sheep until he finally heard its pathetic bleating and rescued it.

> *And all through the mountains thunder riven*
> *And up from the rocky steep,*
> *There arose a glad cry to the gate of Heaven,*
> *"Rejoice! I have found My sheep!"*[6]

The Lord Jesus spoke with deep emotion when He told His disciples in Luke 12:32, "Do not fear, little flock, for it is your Father's good pleasure to give you the kingdom." Later in speaking to Peter along the shoreline of Galilee, He implored him to "Feed My lambs . . . Tend My sheep . . . Feed My sheep" (John 21:15–17).

John 10 is the Bible's zenith on this subject. "I am the good shepherd," said Jesus. "The good shepherd gives His life for the sheep . . . I know My sheep, and am known by My own. As the Father knows Me, even so I know the Father; and I lay down My life for the sheep" (John 10:11–15).

Shepherding was a solitary duty, and sometimes deadly. John

Muir, an early naturalist who wrote about life in the American West, once described a shepherd in the California Sierras named Billy. He was a solitary mountain man who slept fully clothed in the rotten dust of a log, wrapped in a red blanket. Attached to one side of his belt was a six-shooter. On the other side was his lunch in a bag from which gravy and juices constantly dripped down his leg. These drippings were not wiped off. Instead, they were spread over the surface of the trousers so the garment never became threadbare but thickened with layers of grease, dust, insects, and vegetation. In this way, they became "watertight and shiny."

"These precious overalls are never taken off," wrote Muir, "and nobody knows how old they are, though one may guess by their thickness and concentric structure. Instead of wearing thin they wear thick." Their stratification, he added, resembled the rings of a tree.[7]

The life of a shepherd totally revolved around his sheep. One shepherding family in Colorado talked about the total family immersion in their livestock venture. The day school was out, the whole family would move to the summer range and stay there with the sheep until the day school started again in the fall. The wife of another Midwest shepherding family talked about the way her family moved with the migrations of the sheep and built "a life around the sheep and their needs. We had no life of our own. The sheep came first."[8] While our sheep-raising operation was much smaller and simpler, every shepherd can attest to the daily and seasonal care required to keep a flock healthy and happy.

* * *

Shepherding has been called the loneliest job in the world. One man, Nick Santana, was a Romanian sheep man who took great pride in his flocks and wouldn't leave them even at the cost of his own life. He was caught in a blizzard that swept over the Rocky Mountains earlier than expected. He valiantly attempted to bring his sheep to safety from the mountain range but failed. His frozen body was found among those of his sheep, and his last thoughts were of his wife, his dogs, and his flocks. "I stayed too long," he scribbled in pencil on a scrap of paper. "Made big mistake."[9]

There's a magnetism between a shepherd and his flock that's hard to imagine. In writing Psalm 23, David understood this emotional bond very well. He never forgot how attached he had become to his wooly animals as he had migrated with his flocks for weeks and months in the remote pathways of Palestine.

And it's no accident that the prophet Nathan later turned those memories into a knife to plunge into David's heart after the affair with Bathsheba. It was the low point of David's life. Having risen to the throne, David could have had any woman in the kingdom, yet he coveted and took the wife of a lowly officer in his army and later arranged the man's death. Sometime afterward, Nathan showed up at the palace, pulled the callused king aside, and said something like, "Your Highness, let me tell you a story."

Nathan told David about a poor man who "had nothing, except one little ewe lamb which he had bought and nourished; and it grew up together with him and with his children. It ate of his own food and drank from his own cup and lay in his bosom; and it was like a daughter to him."

But a heartless neighbor—a man with endless flocks and

herds of his own—seized that little lamb and butchered it for a wayfaring guest who showed up unexpectedly, needing a hot meal. The neighbor served the poor man's pet for supper. What should be done to such a cruel neighbor?

David, recalling his love for his own flocks, seethed as he listened and exclaimed, "Any man who would do such a thing deserves to die" (2 Samuel 12:5, NLB).

Turning on him like a sword, Nathan whispered, "You are that man."

The pinprick of a shepherd's love burst the dam of David's hardened heart and led him to later write Psalm 51: "Have mercy upon me, O God . . . Against You, You only, have I sinned and done this evil in Your sight . . . Wash me, and I shall be whiter than snow . . . Create in me a clean heart, O God . . . A broken and contrite heart—these, O God, You will not despise." Like a shepherd who deeply loves and freely forgives, our God is devoted to us, longing to give us a clean heart, a contrite spirit, and a joyful relationship with Himself.

Animal Lessons

When God created animals, He seemed to design some of them as educational tools. By watching an eagle soar in the heavens, we can learn about the updraft of faith (Isaiah 40:31). By observing ants, we can learn the importance of diligence (Proverbs 6:6). We're to have the surefootedness of a deer in high places (Habakkuk 3:19), to be shrewd as serpents but harmless as doves

(Matthew 10:16), and to draw near to the Lord as chicks nestling under the wings of a hen (Luke 13:34).

Sheep are mentioned more than any other animal in Scripture to teach us about ourselves, but the primary lesson is this: we need a lifelong shepherd, one who loves us and whom we can love in return. The tender affection between sheep and shepherd is a picture of our own relationship with our Lord Jesus Christ.

One winter at our house, our shepherding duties drew to a close. Our little flock had died off from old age, one by one, until only Lucy was left. She'd been bottle-fed as a lamb, had frolicked as a youngling, and had enjoyed a lifetime of safe grazing and frequent fellowship in the back pasture. But our daughters had grown up and moved away. Lucy had become my responsibility, and I fretted at her increasing feebleness and frailty.

Every day I'd try to go down to the field, feed her oats out of my hand, tickle and rub her ears, and replenish her water. We became attached; and when she grew ill, I was nearly as troubled as if she were a person. Her wool became as thin as a threadbare coat, and I worried about her getting cold on frosty nights. She didn't want to stay in the little barn, so I made her a warm place among the hay bales. One evening in early January, the temperatures plunged. I tried to keep Lucy warm with blankets and hay. But the next morning she had trouble getting on her feet. She lay in her little sheltered bed and looked up at me with apprehension in her nearly sightless eyes.

I called a friend who worked for a veterinarian, and with a livestock stretcher we carried her to the barn. Finding a long power cord, I ran a heater to her stall and kept her covered with blankets. Every day I'd go down to the little barn, sit down beside her, cradle her old wooly head in my lap, and talk to her. She seemed to like that. I tried to get her to eat and drink, but she didn't want anything. I sang to her ("Savior, Like a Shepherd Lead Us"), and I prayed for her and asked the Lord to help her. She seemed comforted by those visits, and I was loath to leave. As a pastor, I've made many visits to hospital rooms, and this was similar. In some ways it was even more personal, for this was someone I'd known for years and for whom I was responsible as a shepherd.

Lucy wasn't able to recover. She was just too old. The day came when I had to depart on an overseas trip, and I asked my son-in-law, Ethan, if he would take care of her. I couldn't say more than that, but he knew what I meant. He was with her at the end and saw that she was cared for and buried near her erstwhile companions in the pasture that had been her lifelong home.

Looking back on the experience, I'm surprised at the grief I felt and still feel. It's hard to explain the affection between a shepherd and his sheep, but this gave me a glimpse into the depth of feelings that we share with our God whenever we say "The Lord is my Shepherd." The Lord is not just *a* shepherd or *the* shepherd. He is *my* shepherd and He is *your* shepherd. We are His people, the sheep of His pasture.

> O this full and perfect peace! O this transport all divine!
> In a love which cannot cease, I am His, and He is mine.
> —George W. Robinson, 1876

To believe the Twenty-third Psalm

is to live a life of victory, a life of joy and peace,

a life triumphant in prayer, in Bible study, in service.

—DR. ROBERT C. MCQUILKIN[1]

3

"Shepherd"

PSALM 23:1

$\mathcal{A}$llan C. Emery was a successful industrialist whose keen insights made him an invaluable advisor to the evangelist Billy Graham and to the many colleges, universities, and philanthropic organizations on whose boards he sat. In his autobiography, *A Turtle on a Fencepost,* he told of an interesting experience that impressed him as a young man. Allan began his career working with his father in the wool business and once spent an evening with a shepherd on the Texas prairie. The shepherd had dogs to help him herd and protect the sheep, but he was the only person in charge.

It was in the springtime of the year, and the snows had only recently melted. The grass was turning green. There were about two thousand sheep in a large flock, and the shepherd built a large bonfire. Allan drank in the scene as if it were a page in a picture book—one shepherd, three sheep dogs, a bonfire, and two thousand sheep. As the night wore on, the sheep settled down and all was quiet until suddenly the long, loud wail of coyotes pierced the air. The dogs growled and peered into the darkness. The sheep, which had been sleeping, lumbered to their feet, alarmed, bleating pitifully. The shepherd tossed more logs onto the fire, and the flames shot up.

In the glow, Allan looked out and saw thousands of little lights. He realized those were reflections of the fire in the eyes of the sheep. Those sheep had instinctively looked toward the shepherd. "In the midst of danger," Allan observed, "the sheep were not looking out into the darkness but were keeping their eyes set in the direction of their safety, looking toward the shepherd. I couldn't help but think of Hebrews 12: ' . . . looking unto Jesus, the author and finisher of our faith. . . . ' "[2]

What a picture of faith. It's predicated by the fact that sheep are the most helpless creatures on earth. Dogs can run in packs, hunt for food, find their ways when lost, and defend themselves when attacked. Cats of all sizes are stubborn, solitary creatures with minds of their own. They prowl and pounce. Horses, though capable of domestication and harnessing, are noble in wild herds thundering across the plains. Even cattle can roam on the wild prairie. Rabbits, birds, reptiles, fish, and monkeys can be found in pet stores but are happiest in the wild. The forests and jungles of the world are full of wildlife requiring no human care. These animals require no specialized care by a shepherd, but we're not like them: we're sheep. And by understanding the shepherd's role in our lives, we better comprehend our own makeup and upkeep.

A sheep is the one animal that is utterly clueless and helpless without a human being nearby. A flock of sheep without a shepherd is a pathetic sight. You never hear of sheep migrating along in great flocks, fending for themselves, or surviving without external protection. They panic at the slightest sound. They have no sense of direction, little native intelligence, and no way to defend themselves. They can butt a little with their heads, but they're bulky, bungling, and without defensive equipment. They can't fight with their hooves or teeth. They can't run away very easily, or dig holes or climb trees. They can't track down their own food. They can get lost even in their own pasture. Their wool, which becomes thick, matted, and tangled if not regularly sheared, can weigh them down or trap them in thorns. Insects bedevil them, and they don't recover well from disease and injury unless treated individually. Sheep also need affection, and there's something about them that seems to crave human care. They are utterly dependent on a shepherd.

They're just like us. We might think we can get along just fine without a good and gracious God, and many people deny and discredit Him. But in the end, we're nothing more than sheep without a shepherd when we distance ourselves from a loving Creator. We're defenseless against the prowling lion that wants to devour us. We're lost without someone to show us the path. We'll starve without a prepared pasture. We're easily diseased and often frightened. Without someone tending us, we become ragged, unhealthy, and utterly pathetic.

That's why the second phrase in Psalm 23 is vital. It sets the stage for the remaining words in the Shepherd's Song, and it sums up the theme of the whole poem: *The Lord is my Shepherd; I shall not want.*

Of course, the word *want* is used in its archaic sense here. It doesn't mean that if the Lord's our Shepherd we'll have everything we *want*. It means we'll not *want* for anything we *need*. Our English word *want* comes from a medieval term meaning "to be abandoned," and in the days of the King James Version, it had to do with our essential needs.

I've always liked the way the Living Bible put it: "Because the Lord is my shepherd, I have everything I need."

That's the theme of Psalm 23. Yes, the green pastures and dark valleys and high tablelands are all there, and the imagery is rich and meaningful. But in essence, the remaining five verses of the psalm are simply a list of the implications and outworkings of verse 1. This is the key to understanding Psalm 23. If it were a sermon (which it is), verse 1 would be the text; verses 2 through 6 would be the exposition.

In essence, the psalmist is saying, "Because the Lord is my shepherd, I shall not lack anything":

- I will not lack peace, for He makes me lie down in green pastures.

- I will not lack provision, for He leads me by still waters.

- I will not lack hope and encouragement, for He restores my soul.

- I will not lack guidance, for He leads me in paths of righteousness for His Name's sake.

- I will not lack deliverance in tough times; for even when I walk through the valley of the shadow of death, I will fear no evil.

- I will not lack companionship, for You are with me.

- I will not lack protection, for Your rod and staff comfort me, and You prepare a table for me in the presence of my enemies.

- I will not lack help and healing in all the events of life, for You anoint my head with oil.

- I will not lack an abundant life, for my cup overflows.

- I will never lack anything, for goodness and mercy follow me all the days of my life.

- I will not lack an eternal, heavenly home, for I will dwell in the house of the Lord forever.

—ternal Needs

This is a frequently given Bible assurance, for Jesus said the same thing in another way in Matthew 6:32–33: "Your heavenly Father knows that you need all these things. But seek first the kingdom of God and His righteousness, and all these things will be added to you."

When David Ben-Gurion, the first prime minister of Israel, was facing a series of existential crises to his young nation, someone asked him what he needed. He said, "The only things we need are things which begin with the letter 'A.'" Then he went on to explain: "A lot of tanks. A lot of money. A lot of guns. A lot of food."[3]

Similarly, all of *our* needs end with six letters: —*ternal,* and the Lord meets every one of these —*ternal* needs.

- He meets our *Ex*ternal needs: food, clothing, provisions, finances, the necessities of life.

- He meets our *E*ternal needs: a relationship with God, salvation, heaven, everlasting life.

- He also meets our *In*ternal needs: love, meaning, purpose, friendship, peace, reassurance, resilience, courage.

During His ministry on earth, Jesus specialized in meeting —ternal needs. He provided fish and bread for the hungry multitudes (external); He reassured the disciples, "Peace I leave with you" (internal); and He told us all that whoever believed in Him should not perish but have everlasting life (eternal).

One of the sweetest categories of promises in the Bible involves His assurance of the multiple provisions we need. Psalm 34:9–10 (NIV) says, "Fear the Lord, you his holy people, for those who fear Him lack nothing. The lions may grow weak and hungry, but those who seek the Lord lack no good thing."

Romans 8:32 says, "He who did not spare His own Son, but delivered Him up for us all, how shall He not with Him also freely give us all things?"

The patriarch Jacob testified, "God has been gracious to me and I have all I need" (Genesis 33:11, NIV).

Psalm 37 says, "I have been young, and now am old; yet I

have not seen the righteous forsaken, nor his descendants begging bread."

The apostle Paul assured us in Philippians 4:19: "And my God shall supply all your need according to His riches in glory by Christ Jesus." In 2 Corinthians 9:8, he affirmed, "God is able to bless you abundantly, so that in all things at all times, having all that you need, you will abound in every good work" (NIV).

According to Psalm 84:11, "No good thing will He withhold from those who walk uprightly."

In 2 Corinthians 9:8, we have a promise punctuated with *all*s: "God is able to make all grace abound toward you, that you, always having all sufficiency in all things, may have an abundance for every good work."

What kinds of needs worry you? What keeps you awake at night? All of our anxieties are somehow related to an unfilled need or the fears of unmet needs.

Last night I slept fitfully, and I think part of the reason was a lurking fear that the complications of my wife's multiple sclerosis are worsening, particularly due to our insurance company's denial of a particular medication she was taking. I fretted not only about her but also about me. As a caregiver, I wondered what would happen to her should something happen to me, and what will happen to me if her condition significantly deteriorates. We sheep are full of apprehensions, aren't we? Without our Shepherd, we're clueless. With Him, we have more than clues; we have Christ. His presence imparts reassurance at every step. So after a night of fretting, I wasn't surprised this morning when I came to Isaiah 12:2 in my daily Bible reading: "Behold, God is my salvation, I will trust and not be afraid."

There's a similar statement in Psalm 56:3: "Whenever I am afraid, I will trust in You." But Isaiah 12:2 takes us to an even healthier level of maturity. It's one thing to trust when we are afraid, but it's even better to trust and not be afraid. This morning I reminded myself that our Shepherd can be fully trusted. We'll never face a need that God doesn't meet, or a day that He doesn't bless, or a situation that He doesn't work all things for our good and His glory.

Everything is summed up in Psalm 23:1 and in its imagery of God's shepherding care: "Because the Lord is my shepherd, I have everything that I need."

When Things Go Wrong

While working on this book, I came across a small poem I clipped out for one of my daughters. Like so many in this economy, she and her family are facing heavy financial burdens, including the aftermath of a wreck that totaled their vehicle. This anonymous poem was inserted into the *Congressional Record* on September 28, 1998, by Representative Dan Burton of Indiana as a tribute to his mother who had just passed away.

Burton spoke of his mother's hard life, of her abusive husband, of her laborious job as waitress in a tearoom, of her selfless love and nurture. Then he said that during some of the hardest days, she made her children memorize many poems, and one particular poem has given him strength and courage during difficult times ever since. He quoted it in his tribute on the floor of the United States House of Representatives.

> *When things go wrong, as they sometimes will,*
> *When the road you're trudging seems all uphill,*
> *When the funds are low, and the debts are high,*
> *And you want to smile, but have to sigh,*
> *When care is pressing you down a bit*
> *Rest if you must, but do not quit.*[4]

That's a noble and simple verse—stoic advice, and good—but this philosophy only works when it's connected to another poem that says "The Lord is my Shepherd; I shall not want." To keep going in tough times, we need an unfailing Promise behind our perseverance and an unfailing Person leading the way who *knows* the way.

That Person is our Shepherd, and His assurance is in Psalm 23: *Because of Jehovah-Roi, I have all I need.* When funds are low and the cares are pressing, we can rest in Him and never quit. When coyotes howl in the night or trouble threatens our peace, we shouldn't peer fearfully into the darkness, but look confidently to the Shepherd, to Jesus, the author and finisher of our faith.

Henry Baker captured this beautifully in 1868, when he wrote and published one of my favorite Psalm 23–related hymns. It says:

> *The King of love my Shepherd is,*
> *Whose goodness faileth never,*
> *I nothing lack if I am His*
> *And He is mine forever.*

Where streams of living water flow
My ransomed soul He leadeth,
And where the verdant pastures grow,
With food celestial feedeth.

Perverse and foolish oft I strayed,
But yet in love He sought me,
And on His shoulder gently laid,
And home, rejoicing, brought me.

In death's dark vale I feel no ill
With Thee, dear Lord, beside me;
Thy rod and staff my comfort still,
Thy cross before to guide me.

Thou spread'st a table in my sight;
Thy unction grace bestoweth;
And O what transport of delight
From Thy pure chalice floweth!

And so through all the length of days
Thy goodness faileth never;
Good Shepherd, may I sing Thy praise
Within Thy house forever.

Part 2

I Shall
Not Want

The Lord is my shepherd;
that's all I want.

—Dr. Robert C. McQuilkin[1]

4

His Peace in Life's Meadows

HE MAKES ME TO LIE DOWN IN GREEN PASTURES; HE LEADS ME BESIDE THE STILL WATERS.

*B*aby boomers like me grew up in the era of television Westerns, and I wish I had a dollar for every episode I've seen of *Wagon Train*, *Rawhide*, *The Lone Ranger*, *Have Gun Will Travel*, Roy Rogers, and *Bonanza*. Some of my earliest memories are sitting on my dad's lap watching black-and-white half-hour episodes of *Gunsmoke* on Saturday nights after my mom had gone to bed.

Cowpunchers were our heroes in those days, and they showed us how to stand up to gunslingers, survive the elements, and ride herd on the cattle drives until we made it to Dodge City or Sacramento. We walked the streets of Laredo, visited the West Texas town of El Paso, passed through the Red River Valley, and were happiest when back in the saddle again.

But something was missing from all those Western television programs and movies—sheep. How many times have we seen flocks of sheep on the Santa Fe Trail? The Marlboro Man was the epitome of tough individualism, but why didn't the Westerns give us stories about the shepherds herding their flocks in the High Sierras? There were more sheep than cattle in those days. The first census of livestock, taken two years after the Civil War, showed 46.3 million sheep compared to a measly 28.5 million head of cattle.[2]

Many of today's western highways were originally sheep routes, and some of our greatest cities (such as San Antonio) based their economies largely on the production of sheep.

You may be surprised to learn that the greatest conflicts in the Wild West weren't between outlaws and lawmen or between cowboys and Indians. They were between cattlemen and the sheepherders who were fighting over pastures for their animals. The Western states were torn apart by the Sheep Wars of the late 1800s, and the major players were just as colorful as Billy the Kid and Wyatt Earp.

"Diamondfield" Jack Davis, for example, was a gunman with a thick handlebar mustache hired by the cattlemen to kill sheepherders. His nickname came from his prospecting for diamonds in Silver City, Idaho, but he was best known for shooting sheepherders dead, using .44 caliber bullets fired from a .45 caliber gun. Though he was captured, convicted, and three times scheduled to be hanged, he escaped the noose each time.[3]

The Tonto Basin War between the Tewksbury family (sheepherders) and the Graham family (cattlemen) lasted five years and resulted in thirty-three deaths. According to Zane Grey's fictionalized version, *To the Last Man,* the war ended only when the males of both families had been killed off.

The combined violence of the Sheep Wars is hard to imagine.

In 1884, cowboys in Arizona ran 100 wild horses into a flock of 25,000 sheep that had bedded down for the night. The ensuing panic stampeded the sheep, and 4,000 of them perished in the quicksand along the river.

In Brown County, Texas, Charles Hanna, who had started sheepherding right after the Civil War, went out to his rock coral one morning to find all 300 of his sheep with their throats slit. In Bent County, Colorado, cowmen poisoned 234 of Jeremiah Booth's prized Cotswold sheep. In 1884, a flock of 1,500 sheep was attacked by cowmen in Garfield County, Colorado, with only a single crippled sheep surviving. In 1904, Wyoming cowboys chased 500 sheep over a high cliff in the Big Horn Valley.[4]

In 1902, a historian of the Sheep Wars wrote that in the previous ten years, cowboys had killed 600,000 sheep, and, he claimed, "five hundred man-killings have annually accompanied the sheep-killing." Most historians consider those figures exaggerated, but maybe not by much. Men were knifed and gunned down. Sheep were burned, stampeded, drowned, poisoned, blown up, run off cliffs, set upon by dogs, and butchered by the thousands. One daughter of a pioneer Oregon sheep man said the only time she saw her father cry was looking at huge piles of his slaughtered sheep.[5]

The lesson from this saga of American history is that pasture-lands are invaluable, and it's also more proof that a good shepherd will defend his grazing lands at all costs. Sheep and horses graze much more closely than cattle; and when a pasture is overgrazed, wind and water erosion can ruin the fields. Cowboys often got on their high horses about this issue, which led to the conflicts. But no one knows a pasture better than a shepherd does, and a great portion of his time is devoted to finding and maintaining present and future grazing lands for his flocks. A good shepherd is constantly preoccupied with pasture acquisition and management. One publication suggested that shepherds think of themselves primarily as grass farmers, because a good pasture is the cornerstone of an effective sheep operation.[6]

It was no different in Bible times. Consider this little paragraph tucked among the genealogical listings of 1 Chronicles 4: "The men whose names are listed came in the days of Hezekiah king of Judah. They attacked the Hamites in their dwellings and also the Meunites who were there and completely destroyed them, as is evident to this day. They then settled in their place, because there was pasture for their flocks" (v. 41, NIV 1984).

In raising our little backyard brood, we never encountered any Sheep Wars, but I did worry one summer when we packed too many animals onto the field just as a drought hit. At one point we had two horses (I'd finally broken down and bought one for the girls while offering to board another for a friend) and four or five head of sheep. Every morning when I inspected the field, I saw less grass and more dirt. By the end of the summer, I was running all over the region in borrowed trucks buying and hauling hay to keep the animals alive.

Much of the stress of shepherding comes from maintaining adequate and rich pasturelands, for sheep will never be healthier than the meadows on which they graze. So when the psalmist said, "He makes me lie down in green pastures," that isn't a trite phrase. The word *green* signifies verdant and rich pasture, as opposed to scruffy and weed infested. It represents diligent, pain-staking care on the part of a wise shepherd to raise a healthy flock by locating and cultivating high quality pasturelands.

This is a biblical metaphor with layers of significance. Psalm 23 is an allegory. We're not talking about real sheep or a real shepherd; we're talking about a beautiful oil painting that hangs in the gallery of our minds to illustrate real truth. We're obviously not animals with four hoofs. Though some of us may be white-haired, we're not covered with wool. When we open our mouths we don't bleat, we speak, even if some of our words come out baaaaadly. David wasn't saying we *are* sheep, but we are *like* sheep. He was painting a picture to show us the comparisons. There are parallels between how God made us and how He made sheep. There are correlations between our almighty God and a Middle Eastern shepherd. It's an analogy we have to interpret along the way.

So while these four words in verse 2—green pastures, still waters—conjure up a beautiful scene in our minds, what exactly is the meaning of it? What lessons can we draw from it? It's not hard to interpret. There are three levels of meaning.

This Is a Picture of Provision: Our Needs Are Met

First, the green pastures and still waters create a picture of provision, telling us that our needs are met. We have a God who knows and meets our needs as thoroughly as a shepherd cares for his flock. Psalm 23:2 follows Psalm 23:1 in a logical way. Because the

Lord is my shepherd, I have everything I need. Specifically, I have green pastures. And I have cool ponds of still water. My needs are met. There are provisions and supplies for my hunger and thirst, and my Shepherd has seen to it that everything I need has been provided—internally, externally, and eternally. Jesus said, "If anyone enters by Me, he will be saved, and will go in and out and find pasture . . . life . . . more abundantly" (John 10:9–11).

This is the significance of the words, "He makes me to *lie down* in green pastures." This doesn't mean that an old ewe, for example, notices that she has plenty to eat as she's about to graze. It means that she has already grazed till she is full, and now she's going to lie down and chew her cud.

Sheep eat while standing on all fours. The only time we had a sheep eat lying down was when she was sick. If I saw a sheep lying down and trying to graze on some grass while she rested her chin on the ground, I worried. A healthy sheep would never eat except while standing upright. If I had a sick sheep, I'd typically find her lying down and eating nothing. Frequently, one of the girls or I would sit down beside her with some sweet feed and try to coax her to nibble by hand, usually with little success.

But after a healthy sheep has stood on all fours through the early morning hours, filling herself with rich, dew-coated herbage, she lies down and begins to chew her cud. Sheep belong to the ruminant class of mammals (there are about 150 similar species, including deer, buffalo, giraffes, moose, elk, and cattle) that have multiple chambers in their stomachs. The grass is quickly bitten off at its roots, swallowed, and stored in an empty compartment for later enjoyment. Afterward, when the animals find a shady place, they will lie down, regurgitate their breakfast, rechew it at leisure, and reswallow it with pleasure. This activity keeps a healthy sheep occupied for several hours each day.

Once when I was working in the backyard, my daughter Hannah was swinging on a tire hanging from an old tree. She was laughing. I walked over and asked her what was so funny, and she pointed to Ethel, one of our sheep, lying in the shade under a nearby tree, legs tucked neatly beneath her, working her chops like a baseball player chewing gum. Chomp, chomp, chomp. Then she swallowed whatever she was chewing, and a moment later she burped and started chewing again. This was repeated over and over, and Hannah thought it was hilarious, which it was.

I took the time to explain the process to Hannah, who found it gross but funny. We both decided that sheep must be pretty smart, after all, if they've figured out how to enjoy the same breakfast twice each day.

When the psalmist says, then, "He makes me lie down in green pastures," he means that his sheep have already grazed to their fill. They are full, they are satisfied, their needs have all been met, and they are resting in the blessing.

This is a tremendous and frequently repeated theme in the Bible. If we make the Lord our Shepherd, He'll see to it that one way or another all our needs are met. He will take personal ownership and responsibility for us, and we simply rest in His blessings.

How often do we have great needs that can be met only at the throne of grace, and how often do we find the Lord supplying them in His own way, even as He sent the ravens to feed Elijah in 2 Kings 17? We have all kinds of needs, and the Lord has all kinds of ways of meeting them in His own way and time.

For many years, I've delighted in reading church histories and missionary biographies, and I've noticed how faithfully the Lord has kept His promises on multiple pages in innumerable lives on countless occasions. For example, in 1990, John D. Robb was conducting a seminar in Russia shortly before the fall of the Iron Curtain. The Soviet Lausanne Congress had brought thirteen hundred Christian leaders from across Russia to the Hotel Izmailovo in Moscow. Everyone was excited that after so many years of atheistic Communist oppression, Christian leaders could now meet openly and share ideas. John's seminar was about reaching Muslims with the Gospel of Jesus Christ, and to his surprise the man who assisted him and translated for him was himself a Muslim and a medical doctor.

Later, as John packed up to check out of his hotel room, the man dropped by to say good-bye and to give him some books about Russia. John looked around to see what he could present the man in return, wanting very much to give him a Christian book. But all his material had already been distributed. Feeling a sudden deep burden about it, John silently prayed, "O Lord, what I'd give for a Russian New Testament right now!"

At that moment there was a rap on the door. Opening it, John saw Russian men with a cart packed high with Russian New Testaments. John looked at them in sheer amazement, wondering if they were angels. They weren't. They were volunteers with the Gideons placing Bibles in hotels due to a recent act signed by Soviet President Mikhail Gorbachev that lifted restrictions on freedom of religion.

"We've just received permission to distribute New Testaments to every room of this hotel," they said.

John gratefully took a copy and handed it to the Muslim doctor.

Three months later, the doctor wrote John, saying, "This book you gave me is the best book I've ever read. It's my friend and constant companion. I've read and reread it." When John Robb was next in Russia, he looked up his friend, who told him over dinner in a Moscow restaurant, "I have given my heart to Jesus Christ as my Savior. I've put my faith in Him."[7]

It's no accident that the New Testament showed up at the exact moment it was needed. It's one of billions of times the Lord has sent a timely provision for His servants. There aren't enough books in the world to record all the stories.

Speaking of the Gideons International, my friends Joe and Betty Henderson have been involved with that organization for many years. Joe is executive director emeritus. Recently they told me about Don Gleaves, a Gideon worker assigned to take a trip to the Ukraine in 1994. A local Gideon was driving Don to an area three or four hours away. Out in the middle of nowhere their car broke down. The distributor cap had broken apart, and there was no way to reassemble it. As Don and the driver stood on the side of the road praying, a car passed them and pulled over. A man got out and walked back to them and without saying a word handed them a distributor cap. It fit perfectly. The man wouldn't take any money; he just turned around and left.[8]

Something similar happened to Chris and Jackie Leggett, Christian relief and development workers in Mauritania. They were going to a conference in Senegal, but because of the congestion at the main border crossing, they took another route along deserted back roads through the Sahara. Suddenly their front tire detached from the vehicle and rolled down the road in front of them. The vehicle came to a sudden stop. They retrieved the tire but had no way of securing it back onto the car. The lug nuts were gone.

Jackie and the children got out of their car and began walking down the road in a futile effort to find their missing nuts when suddenly a shiny black SUV passed them. It was new and clean, which was unheard of in that region. Stopping, the driver reversed, pulled alongside Chris, and asked the problem. He then reached over and gave Chris five golden-colored lug nuts out of a bag full of them. He then drove away in a cloud of dust and sand.[9]

Jesus once said, "Do not worry about your life, what you will eat or what you will drink; nor about your body, what you will put on. Is not life more than food, and the body more than clothing? Look at the birds of the air, for they neither sow nor reap nor gather into barns; yet your heavenly Father feeds them. Are you not of more value than they?" (Matthew 6:25–26).

If the Lord is our Shepherd and we're under His ownership, management, and care, He'll see to it that every crucial need in our lives is met in one way or another. All our material needs. All our emotional needs. All our relational needs. All our spiritual needs. All our heavenly needs.

It may not always seem so at first, of course. Sometimes we don't understand why God delays in meeting our needs, answering our prayers, or solving our problems. Just as Jesus delayed in visiting the home of Lazarus in John 11, and in reaching the storm-tossed disciples in Matthew 14, and in arriving at the home of Jairus in Mark 5, so He has His own timetables for our lives. But His delays are not denials. His promises are irrevocable and unfailing. We walk by faith and not by sight. And faith is the margin between our point of need and His point of action. He does things in His own way, which we retrospectively and invariably find is best. As Martha Cook put it in a nearly forgotten nineteenth-century hymn:

> *In some way or other the Lord will provide;*
> *It may not be my way,*
> *It may not be thy way;*
> *And yet, in His own way,*
> *The Lord will provide.*[10]

This Is a Picture of Peace: Our Minds Are Content

Lying down in green pastures is a picture of provision—our needs are met. But it's also a picture of peace—our minds are content. Sheep won't lie down in green pastures or anywhere else when they're troubled, insecure, or frightened. Lucy, Ethel, Triska, Trinka, and the rest of our small flock lay in the pasture and contentedly chewed their cud when our girls were with them. But if other children ran through the pasture whooping and hollering, the sheep would lumber up to their feet with anxious bleating. If a little dog ran into the field barking and yelping, they would do the same. Sheep lie down only when they feel secure, content, and at peace.

When our Shepherd is near us, our minds can relax. Anxious thoughts retreat in the presence of the Lord and His Word and His promises. Contentment comes as we realize that He is all we need and He meets all our needs. That knowledge imparts an attitude of quietness of spirit.

> Isaiah 30:15 says, "In quietness and confidence shall be your strength."
>
> Job 34:29 asks, "When He gives quietness, who then can make trouble?"
>
> Isaiah 7:4 says, "Take heed, and be quiet; do not fear or be fainthearted."
>
> Isaiah 32:17 says, "The work of righteousness will be peace, and the effect of righteousness, quietness, and assurance forever."

We tend naturally toward covetousness, and we have a hard time relaxing when we're not content. We're prone to want what we don't have rather than to enjoy what we do have. We're so often striving for something more and straining for something else. A truly contented person can still be ambitious, of course.

But it's a sanctified ambition that seeks God's perfect will and rests in God's perfect ways. In Philippians 3, Saint Paul spoke of pressing on toward the goal and straining forward toward God's best. Yet in the next chapter, he said, "I have learned in whatever state I am, to be content . . . I can do all things through Christ who strengthens me" (v. 11–13).

For me, the balance is to be found between goals and outcomes. I can be driven in terms of goals, but I'm learning to be content in terms of outcomes. We can press onward and upward, striving for the success we feel God wants to bestow. Yet we can be content however our plans develop, knowing the Lord does all things well.

The apostle Paul's goal was to take the Gospel to Spain and to evangelize Western Europe, yet when his plans were thwarted and he ended up behind bars in Rome, he said, in effect, "I've learned that whatever happens and in every condition to be content; and I can do that because the Lord is within me strengthening my attitudes. I can do all things through Him who infuses me with strength."

The Christian life is a simple life; and a holy life is one that is quiet and contented at its core. In our world of greed, people measure success by accumulation. Christians measure it by appreciation. We're thankful for what we have, understanding that "a merry heart has a continual feast" (Proverbs 15:15).

Hebrews 13 says, "Keep your lives free from the lust for money: be content with what you have. God has said: 'I will never leave you nor forsake you'" (v. 5, NKJV).

The Bible exhorts us "to lead a quiet life, to mind your

own business, and to work with your own hands" (1 Thessalonians 4:11); and the apostle Peter commends those who exhibit a calm and contented attitude in "the hidden person of the heart, with the incorruptible beauty of a gentle and quiet spirit" (1 Peter 3:4).

The nineteenth-century clergyman William Henry Channing provided us with a great quote: "To live content with small means; to see elegance rather than luxury, and refinement rather than fashion; to be worthy, not respectable; and wealthy, not rich; to listen to stars and birds, babes and sages, with open heart; to study hard; to think quietly, act frankly, talk gently, await occasions, hurry never; in a word, to let the spiritual, unbidden, and unconscious, grow up through the common—this is my symphony."[11]

Contented people enjoy the symphony of life. They're tuned to heaven's music. What if you knew for certain that your every need would be met? What if you knew that the Creator of eternity was your best friend? What if you were convinced that a heavenly mansion awaited you following your earthly mission? What if you knew that your life had meaning? What if you had God's guarantee that everything would turn out well in the end? What if you had total access to His throne twenty-four hours a day? What if you had someone who died for you and rose from the grave to give you a life that was more than abundant?

What if you knew that the Lord was your Shepherd?

Well, He is; and if He is, then all those things are realities. Our Good Shepherd said, "Come to Me, all you who labor and are heavy laden, and I will give you rest."

One thing I noticed about our sheep is they didn't run very much. They aren't like dogs or horses that sprint around like high-strung athletes. Sheep tend to amble along at their own pace unless frightened, and they're not fond of being hurried. Sheep prefer a tranquil life, and they're happiest when things are calm. I'm not suggesting laziness, of course, or lethargy. Just contentment.

The word *contentment* comes from two Latin words: *con* and *tenio*. It means "to hold together," which is the opposite of falling to pieces. Contentment is saying, "The world may be coming apart at the seams, but I'm holding together because of Jesus. Though sometimes confused and occasionally confounded, I have a basis for blessed contentment in His compassion and power."

Contentment is the opposite of distress and greed.

It's not the opposite of excitement, for there's lots of room for adventure in our lives. But the anxious running to and fro, the harried pace, the frenzied pressure of chronic stress, the desire for more and more—these are antithetical to green pastures and still waters. The Bible says, "Godliness with contentment is great gain" (1 Timothy 6:6).

Instead of reminding yourself of what you crave, remind yourself of what you have. Build some quiet zones into your routine. Learn the sound of silence. Make time to rest your weary mind and body. Take time for prayer and contemplation. Reduce your wants. Increase your joys. And be thankful.

A great old writer of yesteryear, William Evans, observed: "It is generally recognized as being a very difficult thing to get God's people to thus lie down. They will do almost anything and everything else but that. They will run, walk, fight, sing, teach, preach, work, in a word do almost anything and everything except seek seasons of quiet and periods of retirement of secret communion with God and quiet soul nurture . . . We do not like pauses . . . [but] from the rush into the hush Jesus calls us."[12]

This Is a Picture of Personal Nourishment: Our Souls Are Fed

Lying down in green pastures, then, is a picture of provision—our needs are met. And it's a picture of peace—our minds are content. But it's also a picture of personal nourishment—our souls are fed. Green pastures are a biblical image of God's Word, even as Psalm 37:3 states: "Dwell in the land, and feed on His faithfulness."

Green pastures have long been a picture of personal Bible study. As I mentioned in a previous chapter, our English word *pastor* is related to the word *pasture,* and it has to do with someone who leads the flock—a church—into the green pastures of the Scripture Sunday after Sunday for the nourishment of their spirits. Jesus commanded Peter in John 21 to feed His flock, and Peter later told the pastors working under him, "Feed the flock of God which is among you" (1 Peter 5:2, King James Version).

In Jeremiah 3:15, the Lord said to Israel, "I will give you shepherds according to My heart, who will feed you with knowledge and understanding."

Later in Jeremiah 23, the Lord excoriated the false teachers of Israel because they weren't providing a nourishing pasture (of solid teaching) for the Israelites. They were serving them careless doctrine and flawed truth. "The pastures in the desert are withered. The prophets follow an evil course," we read in Jeremiah 23:10 (NIV).

Jeremiah went on to warn, "Do not listen to what the prophets are prophesying to you . . . they speak visions from their own minds, not from the mouth of the Lord . . . But which of them has stood in the council of the Lord to see or to hear His Word? . . . But if they had stood in My council, they would have proclaimed My words to My people" (Jeremiah, 23:16–22).

Our job is to take the time to graze in the sweet pasturage of the Word. The Bible says that we are His people and the sheep of His pasture (Psalm 100:3). We find nourishment by abiding in His Word, feeding on His faithfulness, and living on His promises.

Ezekiel 34 continues the theme: "I will tend them with good pasture, and their grazing place will be on Israel's lofty mountains. There they will lie down in a good grazing place; they will feed in rich pasture . . . I will tend My flock and let them lie down . . . you are My flock, the human flock of My pasture, and I am your God" (v. 14–15, 30, HCSB).

Let's go back to the idea of sheep chewing their cud. Despite its distasteful nature, it's a perfect illustration of biblical meditation, which is a lost art among today's Christian believers. Meditation is the practice of chewing on a verse we've previously read, memorized, or studied until we digest it. It's the process of masticating a Scripture until it's broken down and assimilated throughout our souls. In this way, we become what we eat. We gain strength from nutrition.

As a preacher, I'm amazed at how this works. I can study a passage—say, Psalm 23—and read everything I can find about it while working at my desk. I can ferret out every commentary, check out every sermon, look up every word, and diagram every sentence. But the freshest insights come after I close my Bible, leave my study, and take a long walk along the river. Or when I mull over the passage while driving, shaving, or resting. My mind works on the verse the way my stomach works on the lunch I've eaten. When you go to sleep pondering a particular verse, your subconscious mind works on it all night. When you turn off the car speakers and think through the verse while driving to work, you see applications of biblical truth you'd have missed without the practice of meditation.

This is the process of rumination. Remember that word? Sheep belong to the ruminant class of animals, meaning they "chew their cud," rumination being the process of chewing on things. When applied to Bible study, this practice yields insights into the Scripture worth sharing in the pulpit or lectern.

Finding enough quiet time for rumination is a challenge in an age of noise, earbuds, radios, iPods, television, and loudspeakers. But all my electronics (including my mobile phone) have an "off" button. The Bible tells us, "Be still, and know that I am God" (Psalm 46:10).

Remember the old black spiritual: "Steal away, steal away, steal away to Jesus!" We have to learn to steal away for stillness. If you'll just give some serious thought to your life, you can figure out how to carve out a little zone of quiet each day for devotional meditation.

In Genesis 24:63, Isaac went out to meditate in the field in the evening. Joshua later told us to do the same, saying, "This Book of the Law shall not depart from your mouth, but you shall meditate in it day and night" (Joshua 1:8). In Psalm 1, we're given a remarkable promise. If we turn aside from negative influences and learn to meditate on Scripture day and night, we'll be like trees planted by canals of water, bearing fruit in season, keeping leaves green, staying fresh and verdant, and prospering in all we do.

Psalm 49:3 says, "The meditation of my heart shall give understanding." The reason is simple. As we meditate on God's Word, our thoughts are improved. We're invigorated by the contemplation of God. We begin seeing things as Christ does, and we are transformed by the renewing of our minds. As we become mentally healthier and wiser, we become more prosperous and successful.

In Psalm 119, we read: "I will meditate on Your precepts, and contemplate Your ways . . . So shall I meditate on Your wonderful works . . . I will meditate on Your statutes . . . I will meditate on Your precepts . . . Oh, how I love Your law! It is my meditation all the day . . . I have more understanding than all my teachers, for Your testimonies are my meditation" (v. 15, 27, 48, 78, 97, 99).

When we're reading our Bibles, studying books, and listening to sermons, we're grazing in green pastures. But when we meditate on what we've read, studied, and heard, we're ruminating. As we chew on what we've learned, we digest it and receive its nourishment. Our needs are met. Our hearts are content. Our souls are fed. We're like sheep lying down in green pastures and enjoying our meal twice.

And Still Waters

That brings us to the still waters. Edith Pouquette, who lives in Williams, Arizona, recently told me about her husband's recollections growing up on a sheep ranch. When he was a boy, Albert used to go with his dad, Papa Joe, out to the sheep camps. The headlights on the old truck wouldn't always work, Albert recalled, so his dad often gave him a flashlight and told him to ride on the hood and "shine" the way for them. After talking and joking with the sheepherders and cooks, they'd drive over every inch of land, checking water holes and fences.

"Papa Joe was a proud sheep man," wrote Edith. "Sheep men are a special breed of people. They are gentle because their sheep require it. They are fierce because conditions are at most always adverse. They are rugged because they are outdoorsmen. They are businessmen because sheep are their livelihood. They are good providers because their families and employees depend on them. Perhaps more than anything else, they are fighters. They fight droughts, predators, bad feeding grounds, inflation, deflation, every kind of sickness and disease known to sheep. Raising sheep is not a business that requires eight hours a day, five days a week. It requires all of one's time and thought if one is to be the kind of sheep man that goes on from one generation to another."

When he was twenty-four, Joe and a fellow herder walked several hundred miles from Arizona to Utah to buy sheep, accompanied by three burros and two dogs. As they returned with their sheep, they had to cross the Colorado River on a ferryboat, which frightened the sheep and required constant oversight. On this and subsequent trips, Joe would have up to one thousand sheep. Since a ferry could hold only about one hundred, many crossings were required. Joe said that he had one friend whose sheep got away from him. They smelled the water from the river and in their unchecked panic, they stampeded and were all drowned.[13]

In my files are old pictures of sheep being herded onto these kinds of ferries in the West, and it's easy to see the unease in the sheep. One picture showed a man in a dugout canoe paddling alongside the ferry to pick up any animal that fell overboard. How long it would take a sheep to recover after that kind of trauma I can only imagine.

Think of it this way. When you go to the beach or swimming pool, how many people do you see wearing heavy woolen coats as they jump into the waves or off the diving board? I've jumped into many a pool, but never while wearing my winter coat. I'm not a strong swimmer, and it would pull me under. Sheep have a permanent wool coat that stretches from their noses to their rumps. They have no swimming capabilities, so a fall into the water is a death sentence unless they're rescued.

Hence the need for still waters. In our backyard pasture, we didn't have a pond or stream, so I had a barrel filled with water. We usually had to top it off every day and replace the water frequently, for it became brackish. In the heat of summer, it often became filled with insects and debris. Occasionally a bird would drown while trying to bathe.

Our sheep would never come near the water while I was filling the barrel with the hose. The sound and sight of splashing was too much for their nerves. They'd back away or run off. But after the barrel was filled and the water was stilled, they'd come and drink till they were full.

Now, if the green pastures represent provision (met needs), peace (content minds), and nourishment (well-fed souls), what do the still waters represent? It's an extension of the same picture, for green pastures and still waters go together to form one picture. The Good Shepherd knows what we need, He provides in a way that gives us peace and contentment, and He takes care of all required to satisfy our hunger and thirst.

Yet in terms of biblical imagery, there is a progression of thought as we move from the green pastures to the still waters. While "pastures" is a perfect picture of God's Word, "water" is often a symbol of God's Spirit. In John 7:37–38, Jesus said, "'If anyone thirsts, let him come to Me and drink. He who believes in Me, as the Scripture has said, out of his heart will flow rivers of living water.' But this He spoke concerning the Spirit, whom those believing in Him would receive."

The correlation between God's Word and God's Spirit is terribly important to understand. As we feed on the Bible, we need the hydration of the Spirit to break it down in our hearts and assimilate it to every part of our being. It's the Spirit that soaks God's truth into our souls.

When we study the Bible, it's always a good idea to whisper a prayer, asking God for spiritual illumination. The Bible says, "We have received, not the spirit of the world, but the Spirit who is from God, that we might know the things that have been freely given to us by God" (1 Corinthians 2:12). After all, the Holy Spirit who inspired the Scriptures is the best teacher as He opens His Word to our hearts while simultaneously opening our hearts to His Word.

The psalmist prayed, "Open my eyes, that I may see wondrous things from Your law" (Psalm 119:18). Jesus promised, "The Helper, the Holy Spirit, whom the Father will send in My name, He will teach you all things, and bring to your remembrance all things that I said to you" (John 14:26).

It seems to me that Bible study and the Holy Spirit go together just like green pastures and still waters. And here's one final thought. Sometimes in our meadow, I'd fill up our watering barrel, but the sheep wouldn't drink from it. During some seasons of the year, I noticed it stayed full and I could go for days without replenishing it, though I'd periodically swap the water out to keep it from becoming brackish.

I finally figured out why the sheep could occasionally go for days without seeming to drink very much. It typically happened when the weather changed and we had heavy dews. During these periods when the grass was sopping wet with natural moisture, the sheep imbibed their needed hydration with their breakfast.

I think it's a wonderful picture of the Spirit-drenched Scriptures. In the early morning, we graze in the sweet pasturage of the Word of God covered with the watery dew of the Holy Spirit. Like thousands of other Christians, I begin almost every morning of my life the same way. Grabbing a cup of coffee, I head to a small upstairs desk to begin the day with prayer and Bible study. Sometimes I do the same at night before retiring. It's like lying down in green pastures and by still waters. Here we find spiritual provision, mental peace, and inner nourishment.

To quote William Evans again: "There can be no spiritual strength sufficient to walk in the paths of righteousness unless time is taken to lie down in the green pastures of the divine Word by the still waters of prayer."[14]

Green pastures and still waters have never been as available as they are to us right now. Because the Lord is our Shepherd, we have His peace in life's meadows.

The Lord is our Shepherd . . .
He refreshes us when weary
and encourages us when we are cast down.

—Dr. Robert C. McQuilkin[1]

5

His Power in Life's Trenches

HE RESTORES MY SOUL.

Looking back over a long and fruitful life, my friend Earl Langley recently told me of a cherished early memory. At age six, he attended a church where a woman named Mrs. Peters was keen on Scripture memory. To any child who would memorize Psalm 23, she offered a pencil with a plastic cover on which was printed a Scripture verse. "I remember being very intrigued with those small shiny pencils," said Earl. "I memorized Psalm 23 and won one of them. But what I really won was a far greater prize—a marvelous passage of Scripture that has stayed with me through all these years. I'm seventy-three now, and while other passages seem to escape my memory, the Twenty-third Psalm remains firmly entrenched there. Praise the Lord who is and has been my Shepherd for all these years."[2]

It's funny how many people can remember when they memorized this passage. I was in the second grade at East Side Elementary School. That was our memory project for the year. I was about eight years old at the time, and that's been over a half-century ago. I've had a fifty-plus-year relationship with Psalm 23, and it's as refreshing to me now as it has ever been. It was undoubtedly the best thing I learned in the second grade, and one of the most treasured acquisitions of my life.

The Twenty-third Psalm took on new meaning while I was a student at Columbia International University in the early 1970s. I heard an excellent series of sermons on this passage by my pastor, Dr. H. Edwin Young; at the same time I devoured Phillip Keller's 1970 bestseller, *A Shepherd Looks at Psalm 23*. I was particularly encouraged with Keller's insights into verse 3: "He restores my soul."

Keller, who was born to missionary parents in Kenya, had a rich and varied career. In fact, he had multiple careers, one of which was raising sheep. Bringing his experiences to bear in his book, he wrote about the unfortunate nature of what the British call a "cast sheep" or "cast-down sheep," one that gets itself literally turned upside down. Sometimes a sheep—often a heavy or overweight one—will decide to lie down in a little hollow or depression in the field. Depending on the incline of the ground, the sheep can easily shift a little too far and get into a position where its feet no longer touch the ground. Weighted down by its load of wool, the creature will struggle, which usually exacerbates the situation.

A cast sheep is a sad being, legs futilely flailing the air, gasses building up in the rumen, blood circulation draining away from the extremities. It's vulnerable to attack, unable to take food or water, sometimes mired in mud and briars. Cast sheep can perish in a matter of hours unless the shepherd finds them and restores them.[3]

There's an old shepherding maxim: "A down sheep is a dead sheep."

The Bible sometimes speaks of people as being "cast down." We tumble into the trenches of life, and we need the Shepherd's power—His strong hands and muscles and shoulders—to reach around us, reposition us, lift us, restore, and rehabilitate us. In Psalm 42:5, the psalmist asked, "Why are you cast down, O my soul? And why are you disquieted within me? Hope in God, for I shall yet praise Him for the help of His countenance."

In 2 Corinthians 7:6, we're told that our Shepherd is One who comforts the downcast.

Are you cast down? Is your world upside down? Are you unable to right yourself? We so frequently need this tiny phrase of four words in Psalm 23:3: "He restores my soul." The Hebrew verb means to restore vitality, vigor, and strength. He reinvigorates me, He revives my strength. He gives us power in life's trenches.

He Restores from Sin

We sheep become "cast down" for many reasons. Often the guilt and consequences of our sins cast us down. Recently a woman came to see me, weighed down by a dense gravitational force of accumulated guilt. Now at retirement age, she described her lifetime of bad choices and wrong decisions. She had gone through marriages, cheated on husbands, broken the hearts of her children, squandered money, and in many ways wasted her life. To a great extent, she even felt responsible for the death of one near to her, though she didn't share the details with me. I've never met anyone so hopelessly cast down by regret and remorse.

Taking my business card, I jotted down two lines. The first was a Bible reference, Micah 7:19, which says "You will cast all our sins into the depths of the sea." When our sins *cast* us down, the Lord is able to *cast* our sins away. According to this verse, He casts them *all* away, and the word *all* has no limitations in extent or duration. Furthermore, He casts them *into the sea*, and it's the red sea of the crimson blood of Jesus, shed for us at Calvary. And He doesn't just cast them into the sea, but into the *depths* of the sea—into the deepest regions, into the bottomless realms, never to resurface, never to be seen again.

Underneath the reference of Micah 7:19, I jotted another phrase: "No Fishing!" This was inspired by a point made by the famous Holocaust survivor and Christian teacher Corrie ten Boom, who claimed that when God throws our sins into the depths of the sea, He posts a sign saying: "No Fishing Allowed!"[4]

Nothing good comes from trawling through the waters of the red sea with a grappling hook, dredging up sins that have been previously confessed and forgiven once and for all. When Satan wants to flog us with the memories of our sins, we must envision that vast, bottomless, shoreless, endless sea of blood drawn from Immanuel's veins and realize our sins, once thrown into its unyielding waters, are gone forever. We lose all our guilty stains.

The Lord is so intent that we understand this that He has multiplied the metaphors about it. He wants us to imagine *visually* and *vividly* the total extent of His forgiveness. With God's forgive-

ness, for example, our sins are covered by a thick blanket of daz-
zling white snow (Isaiah 1:18). They are cast from us as far as east
is from west (Psalm 103:12). With His forgiveness, the charges
against us have been erased like letters from a slate (Colossians
2:14). They've been sealed in a bag that can never be reopened
(Job 14:17). God has cast all our sins behind His back (Isaiah
38:17). He has swept them away as a cloud is swept from the sky
and never seen again (Isaiah 44:22). He has cast them into the
midst of the ocean of His mercy and grace (Micah 7:19).

Memorize some or all of the Bible verses indicated by the pa-
rentheses in the prior paragraph, visualize the scenes they describe,
personalize the promises for yourself, and see how your soul is
restored to joy, freedom, and peace. When the psalmist said, "He
restores my soul," he meant, "He restores me. He restores my emo-
tional and spiritual well-being. He restores my spirits. He restores
my sense of confidence and usefulness in life. He restores the joy of
my fellowship with God."

Henry Varley (1835–1912) was a British butcher who was
converted to Christ and sensed God calling him into the ministry.
He started preaching to pig feeders at Notting Hill every Sunday.
This unlikely ministry resulted in hundreds of people converting
to Christ and in the building of a large church. That launched Var-
ley into a remarkable ministry that established him as one of the
greatest evangelists of his day.

On one occasion, Varley met a man who had lost his sense
of fellowship with the Lord and with the church. In answer to
Varley's inquiry, the man said, "I was a Christian once, but I fell."

"Well, but have you never been restored?" asked Varley.

"No," said the man. "I have been utterly miserable about it and would give anything to be what I once was."

"Would you like to be restored at this moment, for as surely as God lives, you may be?"

The man looked at the evangelist skeptically, not believing he could ever again regain the joy of Christian victory.

"Suppose you had a daughter who had sinned against you and given you great sorrow," said Varley. "Last night, however, I will suggest that she came and threw her arms about her mother's neck, saying, 'Oh, Mother, I am so ashamed of myself for having given you and dear Father such anxiety and sorrow; do forgive me.' Now, I will imagine that you know this; I ask, can your daughter restore herself, or must her restoration be your act?"

"Mine," the man replied,

"Now, how soon would you restore her? In twelve years?"

"Surely no."

"Well, in twelve months?"

"No."

"Well, in three?"

"No."

"Then how soon would you restore her?"

"Why, at once," said the man.

"What?" exclaimed Varley. "Are you prepared at once to restore your child, and do you think that our Father in Heaven is not prepared upon confession to Him to restore immediately?"

Varley opened his Bible to Psalm 23 and asked the man to

read the third verse: "He restores my soul." The evangelist pointed out that the word *restores* is present tense. It's something God does now—immediately. Like a bolt of lightning, the truth dawned on that man that forgiveness and restoration were available for him at that moment instantly. With joy he prayed, confessed his sin, and felt the Good Shepherd lifting him and setting him on his feet. "Thank God," he said. "I see it clearly now. It is God that restores. He has restored my soul. How strange that I never saw that before."[5]

Have you seen that before?

Psalm 40:2–3 says, "He also brought me up out of a horrible pit, out of the miry clay, and set my feet upon a rock, and established my steps. He has put a new song in my mouth—Praise to our God; many will see it and fear, and will trust in the Lord."

The final verse of Psalm 119—this longest chapter of the Bible—is especially appropriate: "I have gone astray like a lost sheep; seek Your servant, for I do not forget Your commandments."

Ezekiel 34:11 promises, "For thus says the Lord God: 'Indeed I Myself will search for My sheep and seek them out.'"

Whatever our regrets, the Good Shepherd seeks us out. He doesn't want us "cast down" when His forgiveness is so available and His grace so eternal. Decide at this moment that you're going to accept God's instant restoration officially. Turn in repentance and confession. Accept it by faith and with gladness. Let Him restore your soul, at once.

As Henry W. Baker put it in the third verse of his great hymn, "The King of Love":

Perverse and foolish oft I strayed,
But yet in love He sought me,
And on His shoulder gently laid,
And home, rejoicing, brought me.

He Restores from Stress

The Lord also restores our souls when we're been under protracted stress. Like sin, stress can leave us "cast down" by sapping our attitudes and energy. I confess I don't handle stress well. In sudden stress, I panic. In ongoing stress, I worry. In prolonged stress, I sink into depression. When the stressful situation involves something or someone dear to me, I can become as "cast down" as an old ram that has toppled into a rut.

I'm grateful that my children generally handle stress better than I do, and I was greatly encouraged recently by something our daughter Grace put on her internet blog. She and her husband, Joshua, have adopted a happy two-year-old boy from Asia. His name is Jude, and while so much of him is just perfect, there's one troublesome concern. He's not eating, at least not much, not enough. He was malnourished early in life, and he's not showed much interest in eating. His weight is slight and his frame so small that the doctors have placed him in the category of "failure to thrive." Despite a friendly smile and curious personality, he only nibbles at his food. On her informational blog, Grace wrote:

Yesterday after watching him endure a very chalky and torturous digestive track x-ray, I was told that Jude has an intestinal problem, a malrotated bowel. Feeling a little scared and hopeful and even excited (to potentially have an answer to our eating woes), Jude and I made our way to the seventh floor of the hospital to await our squeezed-in, last-minute appointment with a pediatric general surgeon.

The doctor came into our little Exam Room 2 and sat down with an expression of nervousness mixed with sympathy and maybe a tad of tentative pity. But he was kind, and he explained how Jude's small bowel didn't develop correctly in utero and about the subsequent dangers associated with this imperfection.

"But," he said, "the greatest risk to Jude was during infancy, and he obviously came through that just fine, so there's a question as to if it actually needs to be fixed." He also said that he can't be sure it's the cause of Jude's current eating maladies. The doctor then brought up something that made the blood stop coursing through my body: "Have you talked with your doctor about a feeding tube?"

Months ago before Jude came home, our international adoption pediatrician mentioned a G-tube might be a last resort if Jude came home unwilling to eat. But after I recovered from the chill it sent through me, I told myself that all Jude would need was a mama to lovingly feed him. "He'll catch right up," I thought. But lately as the last of my Loving Mama Plan slowly shriveled into oblivion, the terrifying specter of the tube has pervaded my thoughts. So there I was in Exam Room 2 in an appointment I hadn't scheduled, with a surgeon I'd never met, completely unprepared for this conversation.

He went on about it for a minute—about how Jude's not on the growth curve, how he's not even moving towards it, about the many issues we've had, the stress our family must be under, about surgery options. I listened. I looked at Jude, who was sitting on the floor trying to get us to play peek-a-boo with him.

"How do you feel about it?" the doctor asked, which was unfortunate because I wasn't prepared to respond to that question. So I did what I'm sure he was nervous I'd do. I started crying.

Noticing the state I was in, Jude stopped playing peek-a-boo and signaled that he, too, needed a tissue. He wiped his nose as I blew mine, lay his head in my hands, crawled into my lap, ripped his tissue to shreds, signaled for another tissue, ripped it to shreds, signaled for another tissue, ripped it to shreds.

That gave me a minute to pull myself together. I told the doctor that it's something we'd talked about at home and that we don't want a feeding tube. Actually, we *really* don't want a feeding tube. At all. But that I don't think we can keep going like this. And that's the moment I admitted defeat. The moment I accepted my loss, gave up my Loving Mama plan.

Which, as it turns out, was just a little bit . . . relieving.

So as I tossed and turned last night and drank my coffee early this morning, I prayed. And I thought. This road, though scary, is taking our family to a new place where pretty houses and cars mean little, where the "American Dream" is a silly ideal, where the real world and the suffering within it are life-altering, and where the Lord intimately, deeply, gently, and passionately carves through our hearts to reveal potential for growth and strength we never *even knew* to hope for.

Words cannot even describe how beautiful that is. And the Lord is a gentle guide, a comforting companion, a wise counselor. And this road can only lead somewhere completely beautiful. And, actually, the road itself, in all its messiness, is breathtaking and restorative.

And so Grace, facing a rut in the road, knew where to find the everlasting arms to lift her up. Katrina and I are so grateful that our daughters work through problems from a spiritual basis. To pray, to seek God's promises, and to find His restoring power in life's trenches—this has always been the secret of the prevailing saints.

When the nineteenth-century Anglican priest and missionary Henry Martyn felt God's calling him to become an overseas missionary, he was deeply troubled at the thought of leaving his home, church, and loved ones, probably to never see them again in this life. He was lonely and melancholic by nature, and the thought of going to India was daunting. But he worked through his feelings from a spiritual basis and found God's promises to be perpetually restoring.

Here's what he scribbled in his diary as he prepared to say good-bye to his church for overseas service. "February 8, 1805: Began my farewell sermon . . . I came to God, having no plea but His own mercy in Christ, and found the Lord to be gracious, plenteous in goodness and truth, for He restored my soul in good measure. The subject of God's promises . . . was exceedingly animating to me."[6]

During times of stress, God restores us with His almighty presence and animating promises. We never face situations that aren't covered by the promises contained in Scripture, and His promises restore our strength. As the writer of Psalm 119 said: "My soul clings to the dust; revive me according to Your word . . . Revive me in Your way . . . Revive me in Your righteousness . . . Revive me according to Your lovingkindness . . . I am afflicted very much; revive me, O Lord, according to Your word" (v. 25, 37, 40, 88, 107).

"The law of the Lord is perfect," said the psalmist, "restoring the soul" (Psalm 19:7, NASV).

He Restores from Sorrow

We're also often cast down in times of sorrow. Our lives are full of loss. Many of us have experienced losing our youthful vigor to the aging process, or foregoing our assets to economic ruin, losing our loved ones to death, our health to disease, our hopes to disappointments. Everything we have on earth will eventually be lost, and loss brings grief. Were it not for the Good Shepherd who continually restores our souls, where would we be? What would we do?

Last fall I had breakfast with a man in Scottsdale, Arizona, named Wes Robinson. He told me he had grown as one of ten children in a small home outside a town in Northern Ireland. He and two of his brothers slept in the attic. The place where he slept was above the spot where his parents met every night to pray, and he could overhear them from his bed. When he was eleven, he listened to them as they prayed together for him and for his brothers. He was so deeply affected by their prayers that for two weeks as he listened, he cried himself to sleep. "That's what captured me," he said of his parents' prayers. Shortly after, he slipped into a little nearby mission church, knelt down by himself, and asked Jesus to be his Savior. He literally had been led to Christ by his parents' prayers.

As a young man, Wes encountered a series of terrible problems, including the serious illness of his wife. He had also purchased a bankrupt company, but just as he was getting it off the ground, riots broke out in Northern Ireland. It created financial and physical danger for him. Everything went wrong. He was overwhelmed with anxiety. To get away from the cold dampness of Northern Ireland, he took his wife to the south of England on a vacation. While there, they attended a little church where they heard Philippians 4 quoted, the verse that says "Be anxious for nothing..."

At that moment, he said, the Lord lifted his load. He was a changed man, and it was a change that lasted. As his attitude improved, so did the circumstances. He rededicated himself to the career into which God was leading him, prayed over his financial decisions, sought God's wisdom for every move. And in the years since then, despite some crushing blows, he has found the restoring strength of the Good Shepherd to be perpetually sufficient.

Not even death itself can keep us in the gutter, for the Lord gives us a perspective on the subject that overturns the world's outlook. I'm often amazed at the eagerness of the apostle Paul when it came to dying. He told the Philippians that he was caught in a dilemma because he wanted to go on to be with the Lord but felt compelled to minister on earth a while longer. He told the Corinthians that he was groaning for heaven, eager to serve the Lord in His presence. He told Timothy he was ready for God to "deliver" him, referring to his imminent death.

My friend Jim Maloney had this attitude. A faithful member of our church, Jim was an innovative witness for the Lord, full of life and always looking ahead. When the doctor told him his time on earth was short, his eyes sparkled, he pumped the air with his fist, and said, "Yes! Soon with Jesus!" He never lost that outlook.

It reminded me of hymnist Frances Ridley Havergal, who,

noticing the distress of her loved ones as her condition deteriorated, told them not to worry. "It's home the faster!" she said.

Writer William Evans said that Christians should have "a cheerful view of death," citing Paul's words in 2 Corinthians 5:8, that we should be "confident, yes, well pleased rather to be absent from the body and to be present with the Lord."

If you're cast down from sin, stress, or sorrow, turn toward the Shepherd. Trust Him with all your heart. He gives us power in life's trenches. He gives grace in the gullies. The eternal God is our refuge, and underneath are the everlasting arms.

He restores our souls.

Our shepherd guides us into right paths,

and He does it not because we are worthy

but for His name's sake. Have you been troubled about

the question of guidance, in great things or in small?

Will you believe now that the Lord is your Shepherd?

—DR. ROBERT C. MCQUILKIN[1]

6

His Plan for Life's Pathways

HE LEADS ME IN THE PATHS
OF RIGHTEOUSNESS FOR HIS NAME'S SAKE.

Edith Pouquette of Williams, Arizona, recently told me about her family's history with sheep. Her husband was a third-generation sheep owner whose father had come to America from France in 1915, entering the United States through Ellis Island. Papa Pouquette moved to the American West and got into the sheepherding business.

"My husband followed in Papa's footsteps," Edith said, "and we ran about three thousand to four thousand sheep. I tell people we moved eighty times in forty years of marriage, because we'd keep the sheep at our ranch in Williams during the summer and then move them to fields we leased near Phoenix for the winter. When the sheep moved, our family moved.

"Sheep have to be just right," Edith explained. "We had cows, too, and they could stay in Williams year round. But each sheep carries between fifteen to twenty-five pounds of wool, and the summers are too hot in the Arizona desert. Our ranch in Williams is nearly seven thousand feet above sea level, and during the summer the sheep would graze in the highlands, and there they would mate. But before the snows came, we'd load them up and ship them back to the south. There they'd have their lambs, be sheared, and enjoy the winter."

"How did you transport them across Arizona?" I asked.

"We'd walk them to the train station—thousands of head of sheep. It would take four or five days. We'd load them in the livestock cars. Arriving at our destination, we'd walk them to their new pastures. But in the 1970s, the trains stopped taking livestock, so we hired trucks, which came right to the pasture. That made things much easier."[2]

As Edith told me of her eighty moves in forty years, I thought of the Twenty-third Psalm. In biblical times, they had neither railroads nor livestock trucks, of course. Feet and hoofs were the only means of transportation. But the itinerant nature of shepherding was the same, and this leads to the most interesting discovery I've ever made about Psalm 23, one that dawned on me only recently. The progress of this psalm follows the seasonal moves of the shepherds of Israel. Psalm 23 is migratory. Why did the biblical patriarchs such as Abraham, Isaac, and Jacob live in tents instead of houses? Because they were always moving with their flocks, going from pasture to pasture with the seasons.

Sheep are not instinctively migratory, of course, not like a bird that finds its way from a nest in Minnesota to its winter home in Paraguay. If a sheep wanders ten yards from its pasture, it may never find its way back. One day we accidentally left the gate open, and our sheep wandered out of the back pasture and slowly grazed their way to the front yard and then down the road. We live on a busy street, and a friend called me. "I just heard on the radio," she said, "of a report of sheep grazing up and down Pennington Bend Road. I wondered if they are yours." We mobilized like a Special Forces team, rounded up the animals, and herded them back to the pasture. They would never have made it back on their own. They were completely lost. But sheep do instinctively follow their shepherd, and biblical shepherds migrated from pasture to pasture following the seasons, just like the Pouquettes moved their flocks north and south with the cycles of the year.

As you study Psalm 23 from this perspective, it becomes clear that the scene is not stationary; it's an excursion. The flocks begin in green pastures, continue along well-trodden paths, thread through dark canyons, meander into alpine tablelands, circle back through autumnal days to arrive at the master's house at the onset of winter.

David would have known the route well, for his ancestors had been traveling this circuit for a thousand years. They were nomadic tent dwellers (read Abraham's story in Genesis), not because they had trouble finding a spot where they wanted to build a house, but because they had to cycle their flocks from pasture to pasture with the seasons. They maintained a portable lifestyle, just like some of today's Middle Eastern Bedouins.

We know from David's writings that he was familiar with the early Hebrew Scriptures. He obviously knew the book of Genesis and the other early books of the Bible. He often spoke of how he loved the Word of the Lord and meditated on God's statutes. He memorized and pondered the great texts of Moses and carried them with him in his heart. He meditated on God's Law day and night.

We can only imagine how David felt as he watched his flocks in 1000 BC while reading the stories of his ancestors doing the same thing in the same place about 2000 BC. David wrote Psalm 23 with such precision not only because he was himself a shepherd, but also because he came from a thousand-year line of sheepherders. Furthermore, his very sheep were probably the descendants of those kept by Abraham, Isaac, and Jacob. Both the shepherd and his sheep boasted of a heritage rooted in long-ago history.

Psalm 23 Retraces Genesis 37

Therefore, David would have known Genesis 37, the story of the patriarch Jacob sending his brightly clad son, Joseph, to check on his siblings and their flocks. The family home was in Hebron (Genesis 35:27 and 37:14), about twenty miles south of Jerusalem along the ridge of the Judean Mountains. Hebron is pleasant during the winter, and, owing to its elevation in the Judean hills, its temperatures aren't unbearable during the summer. But there's virtually no rainfall between May and September, and the pastures grow thin. The looming desolation of the Negev Desert to the south and the Dead Sea to the east are like the twin tines of a pitchfork, driving the flocks northward.

So it was that the sons of Jacob left on their annual migratory circuit, and Jacob, curious to know how they were doing, sent Joseph to check on them. Leaving the homestead in Hebron, Joseph trekked more than fifty miles to Shechem, where his brothers had summer pastures they used. But the brothers had already left Shechem, pressing upward and higher into the hills. Joseph, wandering around looking for them, met a man who told him that the brothers had migrated to the pasturelands near Dothan, another fifteen or so miles (Genesis 37:12–17).

When Joseph finally caught up with his brothers, they were about a hundred miles from home. Being so far removed from their father Jacob perhaps emboldened the brothers to seize Joseph and sell him as a slave to a caravan of Midianite traders conveniently passing by. Having divested themselves of their pesky half brother, the sons of Jacob continued their peregrinations into the mountains until they finally began circling back toward home with the fabricated story of Joseph's demise.

That story was recorded in the book of Genesis, setting the stage for all subsequent Jewish history. Joseph ended up in Egypt where, by strange twists of Providence, he became prime minister. His family moved to be near him during a famine. Eventually, the Israelites became a nation within a nation until Moses led them out of Egypt and back toward the land God had promised the Patriarchs.

Centuries passed. In the days of 1 Samuel, the teenaged shepherd David found himself shepherding in the footsteps of the sons of Jacob. He began in the southern regions of the Holy Land, in the fields around Bethlehem about a dozen miles from Hebron.

As springtime was swallowed by summer, the blistering heat of the Negev scorched the pastures, sending David northward in search of grazing lands for his sheep. As the season progressed, David would have pushed farther north into the Samaritan hills and the high meadows of the Galilee before finally circling back toward home with his extended flocks as winter approached. All along the route, he likely used the same ancestral grazing grounds employed by his family for generations.

I believe this circuit was in David's mind as he formulated Psalm 23. When we first read this chapter in our modern settings, we might not think of it as a long seasonal journey, but readers in biblical times would have pictured it instantly. Long parades of flocks clogged the roadways of the ancient world like tons of dirty cotton balls. Migrating sheep filled and fouled the well-traveled routes of Israel. The nomadic circuits of flocks and herds were as common in antiquity as trucks and trains today.

In New Testament days, Roman armies traveled with enormous flocks of sheep trailing them. Sheep could trudge for long distances to supply the armies with wool for clothing the soldiers as the weather changed. Sheep also provided milk for drinking, and food in the form of cheese and mutton (Caesar's version of MREs: Meals Ready to Eat). In Roman times, a vast supply chain of flocks (accompanied by herders, butchers, cooks, shearers, and tailors) followed the armies. Though you've never seen it in movies about the Roman Empire, each war was fought with a vast sheep-related industry operating a few miles behind the battlefronts.

Centuries later and on the other side of the globe, as the Spaniard explorers pushed into the American Southwest, they too were accompanied by herds of sheep as "meat on the hoof" for the troops. Jesuit missionaries followed in the wake of the conquistadors, coming to establish missions in the Western regions. They too brought large flocks. Don Juan de Oñate, whose wealth originally came from his family's silver mines, left Mexico with twenty-five hundred wool sheep and four hundred mutton sheep. Crossing the Rio Grande, he found rich pasture-lands around the Chama River in "New" Mexico. These flocks became the foundation for the first commercial sheep-raising industry in what is now the United States. Incredibly, this all happened a full quarter century before the Pilgrims landed at Plymouth Rock.

These Spanish sheepherders migrated northward, traveling with the seasons, and some of their flocks were of exceptional size. Governor Baca of New Mexico had millions of sheep requiring some three thousand Mexican shepherds to manage them. Why sheep and not cattle? Well, there *were* cows and horses, of course. But as one expert explained, "Sheep can survive on land too meager in vegetation and too arid to support other kinds of livestock."[3]

As these shepherds pushed northward, the sheep paths became trails, the trails became roads, and eventually the roads became train tracks and highways. Today as we zip along some of the great thoroughfares in the Western United States, it's interesting to remember that sheep paved the way for us, so to speak.

Throughout the ages, sheepherders have been leaders by profession. A shepherd can't afford to lead his flocks into dead-end canyons or into an area with no water or that's off limits. He can't take them into barren wastelands or into a fenced area where they'll be trapped. He can't backtrack with them, or get lost, or wander around in circles. One misstep can end tragically. He has to know where he is going, and he has to know the route. He has to go before the flock, check out the pathway, and lead them in the right routes with confidence and in safety. Without good navigation, the whole flock can perish in just a day or two.

Flock masters in the Bible constantly faced having to find and maintain a series of pastures that progressed with the seasons, were legally accessible to their flocks, and were linked by suitable trails.

God's School for Leadership

It's no wonder that many of the heroes of the Bible began their careers as shepherds. Abraham, Isaac, Jacob, and the Patriarchs were all shepherds. Moses was tending the flocks of his father-in-law Jethro when God called him to deliver the Israelites. King David started life as a shepherd, and the lessons he learned in the pasture prepared him for the palace. In 1 Chronicles 11:2, as the Lord placed David on the throne, He said, "You shall shepherd My people Israel."

The prophet Amos was a shepherd, and the Lord took him from tending his flock and sent him to preach to his nation. The first announcement of the birth of Christ was made to shepherds keeping watch over the flocks by night.

Think of the leadership skills required of a biblical shepherd:

- Foresight: the ability to anticipate the weather patterns and the cycle of the seasons.

- Advance planning: knowing the routes and destinations and when to access them.

- Negotiating skills and diplomacy: with both landowners and fellow shepherds to acquire exclusive rights to pasturelands and avoid conflicts.

- Geographical skills: a sense of direction, knowledge of terrain, an awareness of dangerous areas and needed sources of water.

- Business savvy: buying and selling of livestock, meat, wool, milk, cheese, grazing grounds.

- Stamina: to withstand the strain of responsibility, the loneliness of solitude, and the dangers of the wilderness. Someone suggested that shepherds end almost every day by praying: "Now I lay me down to sleep exhausted by those doggone sheep."[4]

- Quality control: not all pastures are equally desirable. Shepherds had to monitor, maintain, and improve the quality of their annual pasturing grounds.

- Hard work: pastures didn't manage themselves. They had to be tended, rocks removed, gopher holes filled, undergrowth cleared.

- Motivation: it's not easy to get frightened sheep to follow you through a wild canyon or dark valley.

- Emergency medical skills: to handle injuries and illness in the flock.

- Humility: though a tough job, shepherding wasn't considered a prestigious occupation and shepherds were sometimes despised as riffraff.

Shepherding was God's school for leadership in the Bible. It was His laboratory for teaching the principles of management and stewardship. The God of Israel knew that if someone could lead sheep wisely, he might just be able to lead cities and nations and empires.

Of course, when we think of the Good Shepherd, we have a guide who knows how to lead us along each new trail with flawless skill. He leads us in the right paths for His Name's sake. Life is a journey. Our Shepherd has a strategy for every season, and He leads us with unerring guidance every step of the way. He has a plan for life's pathways.

When I was a university student in South Carolina—a junior or a senior, I don't remember—we had a special end-of-year banquet and invited Dr. Charles Stanley, from the First Baptist Church of Atlanta, as our speaker. At that time, many of us were unsure of the future. Time was forcing us to make decisions that would shape the rest of our lives, but how can one make wise decisions when the future is opaque? Dr. Stanley spoke about the certainty of God's plan for our lives and on the subject of divine guidance. He assured us that our Lord knows the way through the wilderness. He sees the future, and He ordains the plans He has for us. I don't recall the specifics of Dr. Stanley's message that evening, but I still remember how reassured and strengthened I was to learn of the Shepherd's role in leading the way.

And where does He lead us?

In paths of righteousness. This phrase has a dual meaning. First, paths of righteousness are *right* paths. They are right for you and me, and they represent those decisions and directions that will fulfill God's preordained will for me. I believe God leads us specifically, personally, intimately, and down to the details of every day.

Second, they are *righteous* paths; they represent a daily walk that is pleasing to God. His plan for us revolves around holy living. Dr. J. I. Packer points out that the word *paths* in this verse indicates more than isolated actions or individual decisions. It implies "behavior patterns that please God because they correspond to His commandments and match His moral nature."[5]

And He does it for His Name's sake. Not just for our sake, but so He will be glorified when others see how marvelously He is guiding and guarding us.

You can't find a more reassuring subject in the Bible than God's guidance of His children. In an uncertain age, when none of us knows what will happen in the next sixty seconds, we're put at ease knowing that our Good Shepherd is the same yesterday, today, and forever. He knows the future as fully as He knows the past. He knows the plans He has for us, and every twist and turn has been anticipated.

Over the years, I've drawn great encouragement from Psalm 23:3 and its cross-references in Scripture. Read the following verses carefully and circle the individual words that specifically relate to God's guidance. Note the variety of terms used in the Bible to assure us of His direction:

- "Trust in the Lord with all our heart, and lean not on your own understanding; in all your ways acknowledge Him, and He shall direct your paths."—Proverbs 3:5–6.

- "The Lord directs the steps of the godly. He delights in every detail of their lives."—Psalm 37:23 (NLT).

- "You saw me before I was born. Every day of my life was recorded in Your book. Every moment was laid out before a single day had passed."—Psalm 139:16 (NLT).

- "I am the Lord your God, who teaches you what is good for you and leads you along the paths you should follow."—Isaiah 48:17 (NLT).

- "I will guide you along the best pathway for our life. I will advise you and watch over you."—Psalm 32:8 (NLT).

- "For this God is our God for ever and ever; He will be our guide even to the end."—Psalm 48:14 (NIV1984).

- "The Lord will guide you continually, giving you water

when you are dry and restoring your strength."—Isa-iah 58:11 (NLT).

- "You will guide me with Your counsel, and afterward receive me to glory."—Psalm 73:24.

These verses have also inspired a category of our great hymns of guidance, such as "Savior, Like a Shepherd Lead Me." How often do I quietly sing those words when faced with uncertainty. These verses and hymns of guidance have been of immeasurable strength and encouragement to me, and all of them are summarized in this little phrase: "He leads me in paths of righteousness for His Name's sake."

The Seven C's of Divine Guidance

So, then, here's the question. If God has a plan for your life and if He has promised to guide you as clearly as a shepherd leading his sheep, how do we discover and follow His plan for us?

Try sailing on the seven C's of Divine Guidance.

1. **Commit your decision to the Lord in prayer.**

Ask the Lord to lead you. Ask Him to have His way in your decision and in the direction of your life. We can ask God for His leadership anytime and anywhere, of course, but sometimes it helps to find a quiet spot as an altar place regarding an impending decision. I remember as a teenager being unable to sleep because I didn't know what to do about college and career issues. The thought of leaving home was difficult. One midnight I climbed to the side of the hill above our house. I found a spot where I could look down at the home place in the moonlight, knowing my aging parents were asleep in their bedroom. With tears, I asked the Lord to lead me, to show me whether to leave home, whether to go off to college. I asked Him to guide my steps, to lead me in the right paths. Looking back now, I believe He did so. He showed me clearly what to do and gave me the strength and wisdom to do it.

On another occasion, facing a decision about a change in employment, I retreated to the beach and spent time each morning walking up and down the shoreline, listening to the rhythmic waves, and knowing that God knew the tides and seasons of my life. I sought His guidance in prayer.

A few years ago, facing a very difficult decision regarding my church work, I slipped away to a state park and spent two days hiking the trails and praying in my room in the inn. When I arrived at the park, I had no idea how to handle my dilemma. When I left, I had no doubt as to what I should do.

Whenever the future looms, you can say, "Dear God, I believe You have a plan for my life. I want to remind You of the promises You put in Your Bible. I want to remind You of Psalm 23:3, and I want to claim that verse in this decision. You have promised to lead me in paths of righteousness. Good Shepherd, will You lead me and guide me now? Will You show me what to do and grant me the wisdom to make the choice that most pleases You and that represents Your perfect will for my life?"

Jesus spent all night in prayer before choosing and calling His disciples. Though we can't devote a sleepless evening to every decision, we *can* make every decision a matter of prayer.

2. Open the *covers* of the Bible and seek Scriptural direction.

This doesn't mean there will always be a specific verse telling us exactly what to do. That's seldom the case; but in the process of fellowshipping with the Lord in His Word, He'll use Bible texts to give wisdom. Certain Scriptures often become helpful in the decision-making process. It's hard to explain, but it's wonderful to experience. As we meet with the Lord each day for regular Bible study, or as we spend special times in prayer and Scriptural meditation, we'll very often uncover some passage that seems to clarify our thoughts or give direction. It helps us know what to do. It reassures us of the way we should go. "Your ears shall hear a word behind you, saying, 'This is the way, walk in it,' whenever you turn to the right hand or whenever you turn to the left" (Isaiah 30:21).

One of the best-known facts about sheep is their ability to isolate their shepherd's distinctive voice. Many years ago, a boy named Anees T. Baroody grew up in a small village on the spur of a mountain in Lebanon. He became a shepherd before attending the Syrian Protestant College in Beirut and going into the ministry. Years later, he developed a lecture that became popular all over the United States and was recorded in a book entitled *The Syrian Shepherd.* Baroody compared his experiences raising sheep with his observations about sheep in the Bible. "In the shepherd's life," he wrote, "we see all that the human eye needs to see of God."[6]

One summer's morning, Baroody said, as he was out on the pastures near his home on Mount Lebanon, a good friend came along followed by a large flock of moor sheep. On a whim, Baroody decided to try an experiment.

I asked that shepherd if he would let me have his cloak and headgear for a few minutes. He did so. I immediately put them on and stood in front of the sheep, after having first dispatched the shepherd into a good hiding place, and started calling the sheep as their shepherd had been in the habit of calling them—"Ho-ho, ta-ta-ta!"

Then I looked back to see whether the sheep were following me. No, they had not stirred. Such a look of fright on their faces as if they were wondering what kind of creature I was. I called again, imitating the shepherd as much as possible. But the sheep did not move. They were still pinned to the ground like statues. Then I turned around and stretched my hand toward them in a coaxing manner as the shepherd does sometimes, but they jostled each other back in fright. Then I picked up a little tuft of grass and held it out for them very gently, but they edged away from me bleating most pathetically.

Why?

We may think of sheep as dull and near-sighted, but their ears are as keen as radar. They instantly know and recognize their shepherd's voice, and they aren't easily fooled.[7]

It's well known in Bible lands that several large flocks were often mingled together in large stone folds at night. The next morning as each shepherd gives his special call, his flock separates from the others, each group following their own shepherd in turn. Thus, the flocks are disentangled in the morning as easily as they were integrated the night before. Jesus referred to this habit in John 10:2–5: "He who enters by the door is the shepherd of the sheep. To him the doorkeeper opens, and the sheep hear his voice; and he calls his own sheep by name and leads them out . . . The sheep follow him, because they know his voice. Yet they will by no means follow a stranger, but will flee from him, for they do not know the voice of strangers."

It's in reading, memorizing, pondering, and searching God's Word that we most clearly hear His voice and gear our minds to His whispers in our ears, telling us when to turn to the left and to the right.

3. **Seek out the *counsel* of those who know more about the matter than you do.**

This advice comes from the book of Proverbs, where we're told: "Without counsel, plans go awry, but in the multitude of counselors they are established" (Proverbs 15:22).

At the onset of the financial panic of 1907, the eyes of the nation looked to the great Wall Street banker J. P. Morgan, confident he would know what to do. On the evening of October 24, 1907, New York's greatest bankers gathered in Morgan's magnificent home at the corner of Madison Avenue and Thirty-sixth Street, and one by one they met with him in his library. Sitting in an easy chair before the fire, the famous financier played game after game of solitaire while he asked each banker for his advice.

Finally, his assistant, Miss Belle da Costa Greene, asked him, "Why don't you tell them what to do, Mr. Morgan?"

"I don't know what to do myself," admitted the banker, "but sometime soon someone will come in with a plan that I know *will* work, and then I will tell them what to do." And that's exactly what happened.

Most of us will never have to solve a global financial crisis, but very often we don't know what to do with the situations that arise in life. We don't know what decisions to make or what directions to take. But as we ask our trusted friends and seek out wise advisors, one or more of them *will* know what to do, or at least they'll know what step to take next. And their advice will merge with the stirrings of our hearts and minds and so become tools by which God shows us His will.

4. See how the *circumstances* are leading.

God often guides us through His providential leading. He opens and closes doors. He brings the right opportunities at the right times. He brings people into our lives or across our paths at the right junctures. He manipulates events in ways that correspond to our needs. Every Christian biography testifies to this, as do the stories of the heroes of Scripture.

I was struck by this last week while reading the book of Ruth. Naomi and her daughter-in-law Ruth had made an overture to Boaz, but they couldn't control the outcome. Naomi advised

Ruth, "Sit still, my daughter, until you know how the matter will turn out" (Ruth 3:18). We can't always control "how the matter will turn out," so we have to sit still until we see how God will orchestrate things.

We find a similar phrase in the story of Moses' parents when they hid him among the bulrushes in the river Nile. Stationing the baby's older sister nearby to watch, they waited "to see what would happen" (Exodus 2:4, NLT). These godly parents did the best they could, and then they placed their burden in the bulrushes and waited to see what God would do.

We don't often know "how the matter will turn out" or "what will happen," and the Lord may not do as we expect. He may do something different or new. He seldom repeats His formulas. But He has promised to bear our burdens, turn the curses into blessings, and work all things according to the dictates and counsels of His good will. He rules and overrules and oversees. He leads us on the right paths, often ordaining or manipulating circumstances to be like signposts showing us the way.

In his *Notes on Exodus*, C. H. Mackintosh had this to say about the story in Exodus 2: "The renewed mind [the Christian mind] enjoys one of its sweetest exercises while tracing the divine footsteps in circumstances and events in which a thoughtless spirit sees only blind chance or rigid fate. The most trifling matter may, at times, turn out to be a most important link in a chain of events by which the Almighty God is helping forward the development of His grand designs."[8]

In his 1893 book, *The Holy Spirit in Missions,* Boston pastor A. J. Gordon told the story of Barnabas Shaw, a British missionary to South Africa. When Shaw arrived in Cape Town in 1815, intending to preach the Gospel and plant a church, he found city officials hostile to his efforts. Barnabas was banned from engaging in evangelistic work in the city. Not knowing what else to do, he bought a yoke of oxen and a cart, packed his belongings, and headed into the interior, letting the oxen lead the way. On the twenty-seventh day of the trip, he camped for the night near a party of Hottentots who were also traveling through the region. The Hottentots explained they were traveling to Cape Town, hoping to find a missionary to teach them the "Great Word."

Had either group started a half day earlier or later, they would not have met. Had either traveled at a different speed or on a different road, they would have missed one another. God ordained the encounter, and His providence led Barnabas Shaw to his appointed field.[9]

"It is remarkable how God guides us by circumstances," wrote another Christian of yesteryear, F. B. Meyer. "At one moment the way may seem utterly blocked, and then shortly afterward some trivial incident occurs, which might not seem much to others, but which to the keen eye of faith speaks volumes. [These events] are not haphazard results of chance, but the opening up of circumstances in the direction in which we should walk."[10]

5. **Very often, an inner *conviction* will begin to develop.**

The Holy Spirit helps us instinctively know what to do. We develop an inward impulse or a sense of peace (or unease, as the case may be) about a given course of action. Sometimes we refer to this as the "witness of the Spirit to our hearts." I nearly made a decision once that had all the earmarks of being the right one. But I couldn't overcome a nagging sense that somehow it wasn't the best decision, and in the end I went with my instincts. Time proved the wisdom of that decision. Never make a decision if your spirit is sending you warning signs.

6. **Contemplate** the issue.

Think it through. God gave each of us a brain, and He expects us to use it to arrive at a wise and sanctified decision. John Wesley once said, "God generally guides me by presenting reasons to my mind for acting in a certain way." In other words, our guidance often comes in an objective rather than a subjective way. We make a list of pros and cons, we think through the issue, and we prayerfully reach a logical decision inside these marvelous brains that God has given to us.

7. **Find your *contentment* in the way God leads.**

If things don't work out as you'd hoped, trust Him with it. If they do, thank Him for it. Remember Dante's counsel: "In His will is my peace."

One day while I was working outside, I took some time to study our sheep Ethel's eyes. They were dull and cloudy, and I couldn't imagine how she could even see through them. Scientists think that sheep have very keen eyesight, but their vision deteriorates with age. An examination of Ethel's eyes helped me realize the importance of the shepherd's voice in providing direction.

Later, after Ethel and the other sheep were gone, only Lucy was left. She became so old and feeble that she was virtually blind. She often ran into the gate or fence because she couldn't see anything, though her wooly head seemed to absorb these soft collisions without injury. I think she could see shades of darkness or light, but for all practical purposes, she was blind.

Yet there was nothing wrong with her hearing. Sheep have very keen hearing, are able to hear very high pitches, and use each ear separately to tune into and pinpoint sound at its source. When I'd walk down the hill toward the pasture to give her some oats or sweet feed, I always knew the moment she heard me coming. Usually it was when I opened the gate. The chain would rattle against the gate as it opened, and Lucy's head would shoot up in my direction.

She wouldn't move until she heard my voice. But when I called her, she would always take a tentative step in my direction. I'd have to keep talking to her, because otherwise she'd get off track. She'd go in a wayward course, so I'd keep calling her: "This way, Lucy! Right here! Come on! I've got something good for you." She followed the sound of my voice and that kept her on the right track; that kept her, in the words of Psalm 23, in paths of righteousness. In a few moments, she'd be at my feet.

"My sheep hear My voice," Jesus said in John 10:27, "and I know them, and they follow Me." We can't see very well, especially into the future. We see through a glass darkly, as the Bible puts it. We can't see five seconds into the future, but our Lord knows the way through the wilderness.

All the way my Savior leads me,
What have I to ask beside?
Can I doubt His tender mercy,
Who through life has been my guide?
Heavenly peace, divinest comfort,
Here by faith in Him to dwell.
For I know whate're befall me,
Jesus doeth all things well.[11]

As I lay one day in the hospital facing an operation about which the doctors themselves had real uncertainty, I looked to the Lord for some message from His Word. The first sentence that came to my mind was . . . "Yea, though I walk through the valley of the shadow of death, I will fear no evil." Those words came as the voice from heaven, a direct command that I was not to fear.

—DR. ROBERT C. MCQUILKIN[1]

His Presence in Life's Valleys

YEA, THOUGH I WALK THROUGH THE VALLEY
OF THE SHADOW OF DEATH, I WILL FEAR NO
EVIL; FOR YOU ARE WITH ME; YOUR ROD
AND YOUR STAFF, THEY COMFORT ME.

"I was wounded in the northern part of South Korea," Marvin Schmidt told me, "but I have no idea the exact location. We were just a little south of the thirty-eighth parallel. I had arrived in Korea as a quartermaster after a twenty-one-day trip by troop ship. I landed shortly before the Inchon Invasion and worked as a refrigeration mechanic and relief driver on a semi-trailer truck. When the Chinese came into the war in 1950, I was transferred to the infantry.

"Since there'd been heavy American casualties," Marvin said plainly, "they needed more warm bodies in combat."

In May 1951, Schmidt's platoon was bunkered down in a defensive position when enemy forces broke through on both sides. "We were in danger of being surrounded, so the command came to pull out. We started back on a ridgeline along the left side of a valley and walked a long way until we came to the end, to a little valley coming into the main valley. That's where I was hit with small-arms fire that shattered both bones in my right leg. I fell to the ground immediately and started moaning and groaning.

"One of the guys asked me if I could walk. When I said no, he told me to slide down the hill and they'd try to rescue me later. The slope was probably seventy feet or so. I came to a stop on a footpath at the bottom of the hill, and all was quiet until I heard enemy voices. I didn't have time to get off the path, so I flipped over onto my face and pretended to be dead. I didn't know what else to do. I've wondered since if the good Lord gave me the idea of playing dead. I kept waiting for a bullet through my head or a bayonet through my back. But it was beginning to get dark, and after searching me and poking me with their rifles, they moved on. I could hear them laughing and talking, but I couldn't tell if they were North Korean or Chinese."

After the enemy patrol left, Schmidt slid himself a little off the pathway and spent the night hiding, trying to tend to his wounds, and smoking a cigarette that he hid by covering it with his shirt. He fell asleep or passed out, and when he awoke the next morning, he saw he was between the path and a small river. More enemy patrols came by, but when they wanted to take him captive, he showed them his injured leg. Since he couldn't walk, the patrols simply searched him and went on. Just before dark, two enemy soldiers came back, and one of them was a medic. After bandaging his leg and moving him onto the path, they gave him a poncho and some water. The food they offered him looked like dried soybeans, and Schmidt couldn't get himself to eat it.

"Then they took off," Schmidt told me, "because artillery fire started coming into the area." That's when things got worse.

"An artillery shell landed near me and exploded, throwing me about ten feet toward the river. A chunk of shrapnel lodged in my neck, and I was paralyzed. I couldn't move. I thought that was the end of me. I lay there all night, but the next morning I found I could move some after all, and I forced myself to slide a little farther from the footpath. That day some enemy squads—I can't remember how many—came along one after the other and found me but didn't kill me. I didn't see the enemy again after that second day.

"They had taken everything that I had, leaving me with only the clothes on my back and two items. The first was a set of hand grenades and the second was a New Testament I'd been given. It was like someone was telling me, 'You can either use the hand grenade to end your life, or you can turn to the Word of the Lord.' I have to admit I did pick up the hand grenade, but I just couldn't pull the pin. I opened the Bible instead. In the front were a number of writings from the Old Testament. One of these was the Twenty-third Psalm. 'The Lord is my Shepherd, I shall not want.'

"I read that psalm, I don't know how many times over the next five days. I tried to memorize it. I repeated it over and over. As I read the psalm, I prayed. I'm not sure what happened, but I really began to feel at peace. I wasn't afraid even though I was sure I wouldn't survive. The phrase that hit closest to home was about being in the valley of the shadow of death. That's where I literally was, but even in this valley the Lord was with me."

On the third or fourth day, maggots started eating the dead

flesh around the wounds in his leg, which, Marvin claims, probably kept blood poisoning from setting in. He also ran out of drinking water. Though the river was near him, he couldn't reach it. "I broke off a branch from a bush, dipped it in the water, and licked the water from the leaves. I had no food."

For seven days and nights, Marvin Schmidt lay between the path and the river, hovering between life and death, clinging to Psalm 23. On the seventh day, he heard voices. "I turned my upper body around and saw a patrol. I could tell immediately they were American. I yelled as loudly as I could. They put me on a stretcher and carried me back to their company headquarters. I was evacuated by helicopter to a MASH unit. "The helicopter," he told me, "was the type used on the *M*A*S*H* TV show with stretcher pods out on the struts. From there I was sent to a hospital in Osaka, Japan, and on to the Tokyo army hospital, where doctors expected to amputate my leg. As it turned out, the doctor who tended to me was from my home state of Iowa. He was able to save my leg, though I was hospitalized for two years, four months, and one week."

A lifelong Lutheran, Schmidt credits the Good Shepherd for saving his life. "I believe very strongly the Lord God was there with me," he said. "I am sure it was because of Him and His angels that I was able to survive. I have tried to count up the number of ways that my life could have ended during that week, but I've never been able to count them all, for there were so many. But my Shepherd was there with me, even in the valley of the shadow of death."[2]

Those seven words—"the valley of the shadow of death"—

represent one of the most enduring images in human literature. To David, it wasn't just a poetic notion. He was describing a real place. As he led his sheep from the folds of Judea toward the heights of Galilee, he threaded many canyons, some of them deep and steep, infested with thieves and predators, riddled with caves, rimmed by narrow trails.

Some people speculate that the Wadi Kelt was the specific gorge in David's mind as he penned this line of his poem. Perhaps he even hiked out to this famous ravine as he composed his thoughts. It's near Bethlehem, and David probably led his sheep through the Wadi Kelt many times, taking them down to the pasturelands of the Jordan Valley during the winter and early spring months. The city of Jericho at the eastern end of the Wadi Kelt is a desert oasis, and the area around it is well watered in winter and spring.

The word *wadi* is a Middle Eastern term meaning "deep valley" or "ravine." I've been taking or leading tours to Israel since 1976, and I've learned to request bus drivers willing to drive us through the Wadi Kelt. Not all will do so. There's a modern highway between Jerusalem and Jericho, and bus drivers want to use that route. The old passage through the Wadi Kelt is narrow and steep with sharp bends and frightening ledges. On our last trip to the Holy Land, I was disappointed to learn that the Israeli government has blocked off this old road because suicide bombers were using the Wadi Kelt to slip into Jerusalem from Jericho. We were able to drive only a portion of the route.

This is the route Jesus would have taken in biblical times as He left Galilee. He used this very location as the setting for His story about the Good Samaritan in Luke 10. In our Lord's day, it was referred to as "the Way of Blood" because of the treachery of bandits and wild animals.

Dr. Martin Luther King Jr. referred to this gorge in the speech he gave in Memphis the night before his assassination. He and Mrs. King had once rented a car in Jerusalem and driven down this famous road, winding and meandering as the elevations plunged from the heights of Jerusalem to the low elevations of Jericho and the Dead Sea. "It's really conducive for ambushing," Dr. King said of the Wadi Kelt. "In the days of Jesus, it came to be known as the 'Bloody Pass.'"[3]

How fitting that our Lord's final journey to the cross was through the Wadi Kelt, the "Way of Blood," the "Bloody Pass." Matthew's Gospel traces the trip for us. In Matthew 18, the Lord Jesus finished His ministry in the northern regions of Galilee and left for Jerusalem, setting His face like a flint for the journey. Matthew 19:1 says, "When Jesus had finished saying these things, He left Galilee and went into the region of Judea to the other side of the Jordan."

In Matthew 20:17–19, we pick up the story: "Now Jesus, going up to Jerusalem, took the twelve disciples aside on the road and said to them, 'Behold, we are going up to Jerusalem, and the Son of Man will be betrayed to the chief priests and to the scribes; and they will condemn Him to death, and deliver Him to the Gentiles to mock and to scourge and to crucify. And the third day He will rise again.'"

Verse 29 says: "Now as they went out of Jericho, a great multitude followed Him."

Chapter 21 begins: "They drew near Jerusalem, and came to Bethphage, at the Mount of Olives . . ." From here, He entered Jerusalem on Palm Sunday. The only route available in our Lord's time for traveling from Jericho to Jerusalem was the Wadi Kelt— the Way of Blood—the Valley of the Shadow of Death.

Because our Shepherd passed through this valley, we don't need to worry as we approach it, when we're between pastures or changing locations or facing difficulty or nearing death. Jesus knows this route well. He has traveled it before. He traveled it on the way to Calvary, and He fills the valley with the light and safety of His presence. He will get us safely to our heavenly home.

Yea . . .

Notice the first word of Psalm 23:4: "Yea . . ." There are no wasted words in this little poem, so that's an important interjection. It's not "Yea!" like we'd say at a ballgame or sporting event. In this context, it means "yes," and it links verse 3 to verse 4. It is a connecting word, which reinforces our belief that Psalm 23 is the story of a journey, not a still-life scene. The passage says, in effect, "He leads me in paths of righteousness for His Name's sake. Yes, even when those paths lead into dark canyons."

When we're in the Lord's will and following His guidance as best we can, we're on the right paths, even when they seem to snake through the thickets or meander across the ridges. We're where He wants us to be, even when we don't particularly want to be there. We're sheep on the move from green pastures to highland slopes, and the Great Shepherd knows where He's going. He leads us even when the route gets rough and risky.

Yea, Though I Walk Through . . .

The next phrase, "though I walk," represents the necessary transitions that shepherds and their flocks had to endure as they migrated to better pastures. Any of us would rather be in green pastures or on mountain heights, but sometimes we're down in the valley. Valleys can be long, dark, and severe. The shadows are deep and the temperature chilly because the sunlight is blocked.

All this is metaphorical, of course. What we're really talking about are real-life problems. Disease and disability. Protracted legal problems. Prolonged financial pressures. Loved ones in crisis. War. Children in trouble. Marriage on the ropes. Loneliness. Addiction. Depression. Terminal disease. Old age. Death.

Every hero of the Bible traveled these valleys. Remember Joseph, who went looking for his brothers in Genesis 37. He was a strapping seventeen-year-old at the time. When his brothers kidnapped him and sold him into slavery, it was the beginning of a thirteen-year ordeal that included bondage, prison, false charges of sexual assault, and repeated disappointment. Joseph's first response was terror, anguish, and pleading (Genesis 42:21). But when he emerged from this valley at age thirty, he was ready to be prime minister of Egypt.

That's the thing about valleys. They may have shadows and sorrows, but they are "through" passages. Psalm 23:4 does not speak of a cave or a dead-end trail. It's a valley, which means it has an opening on both ends. As I said in my book *The Red Sea Rules* about the Israelites who were trapped on the seashore with Pharaoh's troops in pursuit, the same God who led you in will lead you out.

David didn't even use the phrase "though I walk *in* the valley." The emphasis is on *through*, which indicates a temporary state, a transition, a brighter path ahead, a hopeful future. For Christians, problems are always temporary and blessings always eternal (as opposed to non-Christians, whose blessings are temporal and whose problems are eternal). Valleys don't go on forever, and the road ahead is always bright for the child of God, as bright as His promises. There are no cul-de-sacs on His maps, no blind alleys in His will, no dead ends in His guidance.

Notice also that the "valley of the shadow of death" comes right in the middle of Psalm 23. It's not at the beginning of the poem or at the end. It marks the halfway point of the psalm. Verse 1 begins with an idyllic scene—a good shepherd, contented sheep, green pastures, still waters. Then we take to the pathway—the right route and righteous roads—as we progress from stage to stage. The trail occasionally twists through canyons, and some of the canyons are dark. But as we continue reading, we soon realize that we're on the other side of the valley in verse 5, where our watering troughs are overflowing, and goodness and mercy surround us.

What a wonderful word is that little preposition—*through*.

Yea, Though I Walk Through the Valley of the Shadow of Death

Another important word in verse 4 is *shadow*. This is not the Valley of Death. There *is* a Death Valley in California. In fact, it's a national park. But there's no Death Valley in Psalm 23. It's the valley of the *shadow* of death.

Last year when my son-in-law and I went to Italy, we traveled everywhere by train. We stood on the rail platforms many times. Sometimes as a train approached the station, it would be our train. As it slowed down with its brakes screeching, I'd be hit by a shadow traveling ten or fifteen miles an hour. But I was never hurt.

Sometimes we'd see a train coming that wasn't scheduled to stop at our station. It was an express train, and it whizzed by much faster, making the air rush past me like a windstorm. The platform would tremble, and the roar would be unnerving. I'd be hit by a shadow going one hundred miles an hour. Yet I didn't suffer any injuries.

Once while traveling in Japan, I was hit by the shadow of a bullet train traveling three hundred miles an hour. I have to say, that was a little frightening. It was like an intense five-second horizontal thunder-and-lightning storm. It left me trembling just a bit; but as I checked myself afterward, I saw I wasn't hurt. No broken bones. No cuts or bruises.

That's remarkable to think about. A human being—even a child—can be hit head-on by a shadow going hundreds of miles an hour without suffering the slightest bruise.

Of course, it's another thing to be hit by the actual train.

Here's the point of the word *shadow* in Psalm 23:4. The locomotive force of the wrath of a holy God hit Jesus Christ as He hung on Calvary's cross on Good Friday. He collided with our sins. The guilt of the ages bore down upon Him. The sky turned dark; the earth quaked; the angels recoiled in horror. The Good Shepherd laid down His life for His sheep and bore our death full force.

As a result, we're hit only by the *shadow* of death. There is no such thing as real death for the Christian. God's children never travel through Death Valley. Jesus took that route in our place. For us, there is only the valley of the shadow of death. And since Jesus rose from the dead three days after His crucifixion, He's an excellent tour guide (or shepherd) for us when we're in any kind of valley throughout or at the end of our earthly lives.

Jesus said, "Because I live, you will live also" (John 14:19). He said, "I am the resurrection and the life. He who believes in Me, though He may die, he shall live. And whoever lives and believes in Me shall never die" (John 11:25–26).

This wonderful truth turns our perspective upside down. It makes all the difference. The famous Methodist pastor Charles Allen wrote about a woman who collapsed when news came that her son had been killed. She went into her room, closed the door, and refused to see anyone or to accept any comfort. Her minister came and sat down by the bed, but she wouldn't speak to him. Finally, he began quietly quoting the Twenty-third Psalm. When he came to verse 4 and its great phrase of comfort, the woman began mouthing the words and quoting them to him: "Yes, though I walk through the valley of the shadow of death . . ." A small, serene smile came to the edges of her lips, and she said, "I see it differently now."[4]

As we begin to see things through the prism of Psalm 23, we can say, "Yes, even though I walk through the Valley of the Shadow of Death, I will fear no evil." The Hebrew word for "evil" includes more than moral evil; the word can be translated *distress, misery, injury, calamity,* and *trouble.* The reality of Psalm 23:4 removes the element of existential fear from the life of the Christian.

In earlier times, before the days of sedatives, hospice, and the medical advances that ease one's final hours on earth, many Christian periodicals carried stories of the deathbed accounts of Christians. I have to confess that as I've read some of these stories, I've found them strangely comforting.

For example, in 1825 a book was published entitled *Death Bed Scenes; or The Christian's Companion on Entering the Dark Valley,* by Timothy East. One of the stories concerns the wife of Reverend Joseph Berry of Hackney, in London. Mrs. Berry was described as an elegant and energetic woman tireless in her efforts on behalf of the poor. When her health failed, she turned to Psalm 23 and found it "a heavenly message to me." She told her husband, "If there must be a funeral sermon, let the text be Psalm 23:4." And she requested a hymn for her funeral: "The Lord my Shepherd is, / I shall be well supplied, / Since He is mine, and I am His / What can I want beside?"

As her health continued to decline and she was confined to her bed, she spoke smatterings of conversation with her loved ones, saying: "Almost at home . . . my precious Bible . . . I never thought it could have supported me thus, but it does . . . I never thought I could have enjoyed so much . . . I have not an anxious wish . . . It is heaven already begun . . . I am as happy as I can be on this side of heaven . . . Jesus is very precious. I have no anxiety . . ."

Still later, she whispered to a friend, "It is not like a death-bed—it is sleeping in Jesus' arms." Shortly afterward, she added, "It is sweet to die in Jesus. Bless God. My dear, I am so happy, though I walk through the valley."

Then in her final moments, her friends made out a few snatches of words from her dying lips, evidently inspired by Psalm 23: "Valley . . . Shadow . . . Home . . . Jesus . . . Peace."

And with that, she went to heaven.[5]

The Bible says, "Precious in the sight of the Lord is the death of His saints." A valley isn't necessarily an ugly place. I grew up in the mountains, and I've always been moved by the long majestic crevices that cut between the lofty hills. Gorges are called by that name because they are gorgeous. Even the Wadi Kelt is jaw-dropping in its majestic ravines and magnificent chasms. But whatever the valley, when the Lord lights the path, the shadows flee.

I Will Fear No Evil

Psalm 23:4, then, isn't just a vivid line of poetry. It encases our deepest doctrines and most biblical and cherished beliefs about God's presence in the valleys of life. As a result, we'll fear no evil.

One of the most interesting subjects to trace in the New

Testament is the lack of fear among God's children who were dying. Take Stephen, for example, in Acts 7. As the first Christian martyr, he became an exemplar for all who followed him. "He, being full of the Holy Spirit, gazed into heaven and saw the glory of God, and Jesus standing at the right hand of God, and said, 'Look! I see the heavens opened and the Son of Man standing at the right hand of God . . . Lord Jesus, receive my spirit.' Then he knelt down and cried out with a loud voice, 'Lord, do not charge them with this sin.' And when he had said this, he fell asleep" (Acts 7:55–60).

Stephen felt many emotions, but fear was not one of them.

Of course, as I've indicated, my understanding of Psalm 23:4 doesn't limit the meaning to our dying moments. It refers to all the dark canyons we encounter in our migrations through life. But with the Lord going before us, we can trust Him without fear. So let's paraphrase it like this: "Even in the darker moments of life or in death, I will not give way to panic or anxiety. With the Lord with me, there's no room for fear."

As a regular practitioner of panic and anxiety, I can tell you Psalm 23:4 has strengthened me many times. It's the mental reminder I need for the emotional worries I feel.

For You Are with Me

This verse is powerful in its imagery, but also in its grammar. Here in the valley, in the middle of the psalm and at the most difficult moments in a sheep's life, we're awestruck by the dramatic change of the pronouns. The Twenty-third Psalm starts out in the third person: "The Lord is my Shepherd . . . He makes me lie down . . . He leads me . . . He restores me . . ."

Now in verse 4, David shifts to the second person: "You are with me." The whole poem becomes much more personal. It becomes a prayer, and the psalmist is thrilled with the very close, personal, and constant contact he has with his shepherd, with whom he can speak face to face, friend to friend.

I cannot tell you how powerful this is. Last December, my daughter Victoria had a terrible wreck on her way from collecting her children at school. The van veered off the road, slid down an embankment, burst through a fence, and slammed against a tree. Victoria was knocked unconscious, but her twelve-year-old daughter Christiana had the presence of mind to find the mobile phone and call my son-in-law. "We've been in a bad wreck," she said, "and Mommy isn't awake."

As the news was relayed to me, I had no idea whether Victoria and the other children were alive, and if so, how badly they were hurt. I jumped in the car and headed for town, not even knowing where Victoria would be taken. My heart was pounding, and I could hardly think.

At my moment of greatest panic, a verse came suddenly and forcibly to me. It was from a passage I'd been memorizing—Psalm 46: "God is our refuge and strength, a very present help in trouble." That verse sent "calm waves" where shock waves had been only moments before. By the time I rerouted myself to the right hospital, I was functional again. We praise the Lord that Victoria and her children were not badly injured; they were released by bedtime. But to me one of the never-to-be-forgotten memories of that day is the power of Psalm 46 and the presence it describes. Notice how this verse expands, how it telescopes. Every added word and phrase doubles and redoubles its force.

- God is a *help*.

- He is a *present* help.

- He is a *very* present help.

- He is a very present help *in trouble.*

- He is a very present help in trouble. *Therefore we will not fear . . .*

This is very similar to the testimony of Psalm 23:4, "I will fear no evil, for You are with me." The Bible assures us and reassures us of the real and literal presence of the Lord in, upon, and around our lives every day. Our instant connection to Him is prayer, and one of the simplest prayers in history is: "I will fear no evil, for You are with me."

Recently I drew a connection between three additional Bible verses that thrilled me with the same truth as Psalm 23:4 and Psalm 46:1.

The first was Deuteronomy 31:7–8, which describes how Moses transferred the leadership of Israel to Joshua. He told him publicly: "Be strong and of good courage . . . The Lord, He is the One who goes before you. He will be with you, He will not leave you nor forsake you; do not fear nor be dismayed."

What a fabulous, all-inclusive word! Taken at face value,

Joshua was at that moment effectively immunized from fear and discouragement even in the most demanding challenges of life and leadership, for he had the promise that God would never leave him or forsake him.

At the end of Deuteronomy, Moses passed away, and as we open the book of Joshua, a new epoch begins. In the first paragraph of the book, the Lord Himself reminded Joshua of what Moses had told him, saying: "I will be with you. I will not leave you nor forsake you . . . Be strong and of good courage; do not be afraid, nor be dismayed, for the Lord your God is with you wherever you go" (Joshua 1:5, 1:9).

Joshua received the same promise twice, virtually word for word—once from the lips of Moses and once by direct revelation from God Himself.

Oh, if only we could claim that same promise and rely on that same presence!

Well, we can. At the opposite end of the Bible, we come to Hebrews 13, where the writer is talking about everyday holiness in the lives of his readers. Referring back to Deuteronomy 34 and Joshua 1, he tells the Christians of his day: "Let your conduct be without covetousness; be content with such things as you have. For He Himself has said, 'I will never leave you nor forsake you.' So we may boldly say: 'The Lord is my helper; I will not fear . . .'" (Hebrews 13:5–6).

On the basis of Hebrews 13, then, we have biblical authority to claim the exact promise twice made to Joshua and to appropriate it for ourselves. We are told to do so "boldly." We have God's own assurance of His presence with us, even in the battle, even in the challenges, even in the valley of the shadow of death. We fear no evil, for He is with us.

Your Rod and Your Staff Comfort Me

There's one more important phrase in this verse: "Your rod and your staff, they comfort me." In other words, I am reassured by the shepherd's equipment. He isn't ill prepared. He has a rod to drive off predators and enemies. He knows how to club the foes that attack me. He also has a staff with the crooked or curved top, so He can snag and snatch me if I get too close to the edge of the precipice. He knows how to restrain my footsteps, how to protect me even from myself and my missteps.

Whether the danger comes from outside myself (necessitating the rod) or my own foolishness (requiring the staff), I have a shepherd who is watching carefully and guarding constantly.

As Charles Spurgeon put it in one of his old sermons: "Is the Twenty-third Psalm the song of your faith? 'Yea, though I walk through the valley of the shadow of death I will fear no evil, for Thou art with me.' Have you consciously thought of God standing with you? Then it will not be difficult to perceive the presence of God. You will view it as so real that when you open your eyes in the morning, you'll look to Him in praise. When you close them at night, it'll be like resting under the shadow of His wings."

Spurgeon continued: "I wish we could get back to the spirit of the old Puritans who believed in a *present* God always . . . Oh, to feel God everywhere in the little as well as in the great, in our risings up and in our sittings down, in our goings forth and in our comings in. I can conceive of no life more blessed than the one who knows and feels that God is ever present."[6]

If you're in a valley right now, look around. There beside you is the Good Shepherd. He's holding a rod in one hand, a staff in the other, and you're in His line of sight. You can talk to Him anytime and always. You can pray, for the Good Shepherd gives His presence in life's valleys.

The British writer Joseph Addison composed a quaint hymn on Psalm 23 and published it in 1712. Entitled "The Lord My Pasture Shall Prepare," the third stanza says:

> *Though in the paths of death I tread,*
> *With gloomy horrors overspread,*
> *My steadfast heart shall fear no ill,*
> *For Thou, O Lord, art with me still;*
> *Thy friendly crook shall give me aid*
> *And guide me through the dreadful shade.*

The miracle of this Psalm of resurrection
life is the perfect provision
in the very midst of the enemy's country.

—DR. ROBERT C. MCQUILKIN[1]

8

His Provision on Life's Tablelands

YOU PREPARE A TABLE BEFORE ME
IN THE PRESENCE OF MY ENEMIES.

$\mathcal{D}$onald Britt, a veteran of World War II, lives in Temple Terrace, Florida, and tries his best to care for his ailing wife, who is in a nearby nursing home. His children tend to his needs, counting his pills and making sure he doesn't drive. Sometimes they coax a few stories from him about his experiences in the war. Journalist Alexandra Zayas recently captured some of Donald's recollections.

Donald was in the 422nd Infantry in December 1944, during the Battle of the Bulge. His regiment was cut off from air support and tanks, and they ran out of ammunition. Loss of life was heavy. As they surrendered to the Germans, Donald had seven dog tags in his pocket. He and his fellow survivors were stuffed into a railcar and packed so tightly that the men had to take turns lying down while others straddled their bodies and propped each other up, sleeping on their feet. Zayas wrote:

> The train was stopped at a railroad complex after a couple of days' travel when the prisoners heard the drone of approaching planes, American. The prisoners knew their train was not marked. The bombs began to fall. The guards ran for cover.
>
> "All hell broke loose," Britt said. And the prisoners were stuck. Some tried to break vents with their bare hands but instead bloodied their fists.
>
> Then something happened, Britt said. A soldier pulled out a Bible and began to read the Twenty-third Psalm: "The Lord is my Shepherd, I shall not want."
>
> "It seemed like suddenly, in the car, it was quiet and peaceful," Britt said. "And everybody was listening." In other train cars, dozens of prisoners died. But Britt's was spared.
>
> The next night was Christmas Eve. The train had moved along and then stopped again. The soldiers were thirsty, and someone heard what sounded like running water. Someone else heard the same. Before long, they were all listening; they could actually smell it. They asked a guard for a drink but were denied.
>
> One prisoner suggested maybe the guard would be moved by Christmas carols. "We tried to sing them as good as we could," Britt said. They drew a crowd.

Ultimately, a guard told the prisoners to pass out anything that could hold water. Britt took a drink out of a sweaty helmet liner. "Best water you ever had."

Donald Britt was a prisoner of war for one hundred horrendous days and was held in Stalag IXB, a camp for prisoners. There he witnessed horrendous things. For many years, he didn't tell the worst of his stories, but he now wants his friends to know about the night on a prison train when the hearts of frightened boys were calmed by Psalm 23, read in the presence of their enemies, and how by God's grace their thirst was quenched when their helmets overflowed on Christmas Eve.[2]

The psalmist wrote, "You prepare a table for me in the presence of my enemies. . . . My cup overflows."

In using the word *table,* I think David had in mind what we would call a "tableland," which is an elevated and fairly level region, a plateau, a perfect place for summer grazing.

In tracking the progress of Psalm 23, then, we've long since left the green pastures of Judea, have wound our way through the valleys and canyons leading to higher elevations and cooler summer temperatures. Now in verse 5 we're at the summertime meadows where the sheep can be tended in remote pastures.

It requires a lot of work to convert plateaus into pastures. These tablelands don't just appear on the horizon fully developed. They must be prepared, and this groundwork takes years, generations, even centuries, as we've seen by tracing the line of shepherds from David back to Jacob. Families who buy or lease summer feeding grounds must expend lots of muscle power as rocks are removed, trees cleared, brush burned, weeds uprooted, and poisonous plants eradicated. Sheep are highly allergic to certain plants and plant products, like acorns, azaleas, milkweed, mountain laurel, and red maple leaves. Gopher holes have to be filled, and bare patches seeded. It requires ongoing work by the caretakers of the sheep.

Furthermore, these wild and remote pastures are farther from domesticated and populated areas. Constant vigilance is necessary. Predators are never far away. Coyotes usually attack the sheep at their throats, and they tend to select lambs over mature sheep. They first eat the animal's vital organs, and then move to the flank or the meat behind the ribs. Foxes, which tend to be small, also target lambs. Wolves, which usually travel in packs of two to four, go after the larger sheep, as do bears and wildcats. They'd rather kill several animals and eat the tenderest portions of the carcass than kill just one animal and consume it entirely.

David was an expert on predatory foes, as we learn by eavesdropping on his conversation with King Saul in 1 Samuel 17, when the Philistine giant Goliath threatened Israel. Referring to himself as Saul's servant or subject, David said,

> Your servant used to keep his father's sheep, and when
> a lion or a bear came and took a lamb out of the flock,
> I went out after it and struck it, and delivered the lamb
> from its mouth; and when it arose against me, I caught
> it by its beard, and struck and killed it. Your servant has
> killed both lion and bear; and this uncircumcised Phi-
> listine will be like one of them, seeing he has defied the

armies of the living God . . . The Lord, who delivered me
from the paw of the lion and from the paw of the bear,
He will deliver me from the hand of this Philistine.

Only God could have given David that kind of courage and
reassurance. My wife and I own some mountain property in
Northeast Tennessee. It's been in our family for more than a hun-
dred years, and when I have a chance, I go hiking there. The only
thing that worries me is running into a bear. There's a tremendous
overhanging ledge on our property that has always been called
the Bear Rock. As a young man, I used to climb up to the Bear
Rock, stand on top of it, and practice my sermons. But now that
I'm older, I keep a wary eye out for actual bears at the Bear Rock.
If I ever saw one, I'd probably die from a heart attack before it
could attack me.

Some people are "bears" to get along with, as David himself
learned when he spied Goliath making threatening boasts against
the army of Judah. Later he faced a rogue's gallery of foes when he
became king. The memory of how the Lord had helped him as a
youth never left him, and the meaning of Psalm 23:5 seems to be:
He has provided for me a well-protected space on the tablelands
of Galilee, though enemies lurk nearby. He has prepared a secure
place for me to enjoy, though it's surrounded by foes plotting my
destruction.

The key idea behind this verse is God's protection of His
flock. We have three kinds of enemies in this world. First, we have
national enemies. Whatever passport you hold, your nation has
enemies who would like to defeat you. How odd that after thou-

sands of years of trying, humanity has never achieved so much as a month's worth of lasting global peace. Wars and rumors of wars increase with the passing of time, and every nation is threatened by its own assortment of national or rogue enemies.

Second, and closer to home, we have personal enemies—people who we just don't get along with, for whatever reason. Perhaps someone at school or at work doesn't like you at all. Perhaps there's someone with whom you frequently quarrel or whom you rub the wrong way. Maybe they've been offended by your Christian testimony or for some reason felt threatened by you. They may not even know you, but somehow you know you have a personal enemy. Often broken marriages and domestic quarrels pit us against each other. Children and parents have fallings-out. Neighbors find themselves in disputes with no winners.

Some of the worst disagreements occur at church. When I was first starting out in the ministry, I tried some things that raised the ire of some of the more conservative people in my denomination. One prominent minister told me to my face that I'd have to "fight" him on certain issues. He said we'd have to fight about one thing and another thing, that I was in for a fight, and that if I didn't fight with him over these issues, I wasn't much of a fighter.

The Lord gave me words for the moment. I told him I was just as much a fighter as he was, but I was fighting the world, the flesh, and the devil. "If you want to fight with me," I said, "you'll have to decide which of those categories you fit into."

He didn't bother me much after that.

I've since found that many of the people who were critical of me in prior years are, of course, decent folks. Many of them are now my friends, in fact, and time has seasoned our spirits. Furthermore, not all their criticism was unfounded. We've all made our share of mistakes. Proverbs 19:11 (NIV1984) says: "A man's wisdom gives him patience; it is to his glory to overlook an offense."

I once had two men who became very angry with me at church. I met with them repeatedly, and sometimes our discussions were heated. I confess I sometimes spoke too sharply, as did they. At the request of a mediator, I agreed to talk with them yet again, but with little hope of resolving the dispute. I turned the matter over to the Lord and placed an open Bible on the table before me during our meeting. While I didn't quote this verse or show it to them, my eyes kept falling on the text I'd underlined— Isaiah 7:4 (NIV1984): "Be careful, keep calm and don't be afraid. Do not lose heart because of these two smoldering stubs of firewood."

That's a pretty good verse when it comes to handling foes. In His own timing and way, the Lord took care of the problem. Throughout the process, I learned the most important thing in any argument is to stay calm and keep things in perspective, avoiding at all costs residual bitterness.

We must hold our opinions with integrity, and we can accept the fact that even the best of us will occasionally grow irritable or angry. But lasting damage occurs when the disagreement turns into offended pride, which metastasizes into bitterness. The Bible warns, "See to it that no one fails to obtain the grace of God; that no 'root of bitterness' springs up and causes trouble, and by it many become defiled" (Hebrews 12:15, ESV). Bitterness poisons our personalities like a slow-acting toxin.

With human enemies, we must do the best we can and then leave them in the Lord's hands, releasing the anger like smog into the atmosphere of God's grace. I've had to make a conscious effort to do this, but it's a biblical practice. Here's how the Lord put it in the epistles: "If it is possible, as far as it depends on you, live at peace with everyone. Do not take revenge, my friends, but leave room for God's wrath" (Romans 12:18–19, NIV 1984).

Try to get along with your ex-spouse or your cranky neighbor or your demanding boss. If you can't, leave it in the Lord's hands. He knows how to set a table for you in the wilderness in the presence of your enemies. He knows how to protect you. Offended pride, once it takes hold within us, is like having a lion prowling around in the heart. Bitterness is as nasty as an angry bear. They can shred your soul. Let the Good Shepherd handle them for you. On your knees, turn things over to Him and leave room for His judgments to settle the score and even the outcome.

Third, we have demonic enemies. The Bible consistently warns of our unseen foe who would like to ruin each of us. Sometimes he attacks indirectly using temptations such as pornography or greed. Other assaults are more direct, as happened to Job. One disaster after another struck this mideastern sheik like rhythmic, relentless waves. According to Job 1, it was a carefully planned and coordinated satanic attack to destabilize and demolish Job's faith and his life. It was a plot of Satan; and the word *Satan* comes from a Hebrew word meaning "adversary."

Satan seeks to destroy us, and his demonic hosts are more

dangerous than we may realize. The Bible says, "We are not fighting against flesh-and-blood enemies, but against evil rulers and authorities of the unseen world, against mighty powers in this dark world, and against evil spirits in the heavenly places" (Ephesians 6:12, NLT).

But our foes have already lost the fight. In the book of Hebrews, we read that by His own death Jesus defeated him who held the power of the death; that is the devil. In Revelation 12:10, we read that the saints in the last days overcame their foes by the blood of the Lamb and the word of their testimony. The Bible says of Christ, "He must reign till He has put all enemies under His feet" (1 Corinthians 15:25).

On our own, we're helpless and defenseless, but Jesus keeps us safe. Many times He prevents bad things from happening to us. We have no idea how many times we've been protected and delivered by His providential hand of protection. Other times He allows certain things to happen, but in His own way, He always delivers us from them and through them.

In John 10, Jesus said, "My sheep listen to My voice; I know them and they follow Me. I give them eternal life, and they shall never perish; no one can snatch them out of My hand. My Father, who has given them to Me, is greater than all; no one can snatch them out of My Father's hand" (John 10:27–29).

The Lord is able to provide for us and to protect us throughout life and eternity; and His protective watch-care is part of His tending ministry. He keeps us safe in His hands.

Edith Pouquette, who raised sheep in Arizona for forty years, told me that when sheep are oppressed, they become silent as death. I hadn't observed this from my own years of herding our handful of sheep because our field was totally enclosed by woven fence within the city limits of Nashville. We rarely saw wildlife beyond rabbits, squirrels, and an occasional deer. Never in our sheep-raising years did we lose a sheep to a predator, so, thankfully, I never had occasion to watch sheep react to danger.

Edith's experience, however, is different. She's raised so many sheep over such a wide area for so many years that tragedies are bound to occur. And, she said, sheep ranchers have to be visually vigilant because the attacks come silently. "Sheep, when oppressed, never cry out," Edith said. "One night when we were getting ready to ship the animals to the lower altitudes for the winter, our men were sleeping in their trucks among the flocks. When they woke up the next morning, they discovered that dogs had slaughtered about 120 of the sheep. The dogs just went for the throats, and the sheep didn't make any noise. They were silent when they were attacked.

"I recall helping my husband butcher sheep," she added, "and not a sound came from them as they were slaughtered. They were quiet. When they're sheared, which is a rough job, they never open their mouths. They only bleat in the open fields, but it's their nature to be silent when oppressed."

This is why some shepherds employ bells around the necks of their sheep, to alert them if the sheep are being chased. For whatever reason, they're no good at sounding the alarm themselves.

The Bible says of Christ, "He was oppressed and He was afflicted, yet He opened not His mouth; He was led as a lamb to the slaughter, and as a sheep before its shearers is silent, so He opened not His mouth" (Isaiah 53:7).

This was a prophecy made seven hundred years before Christ's death, and it predicted His compliance with those sending Him to the cross. When Jesus was on trial for His life before the Jewish Ruling Council, before Herod, and before Pontius Pilate, He cooperated with them by offering no argument. Had He mounted a defense, the case against Him would have crumbled. His enemies resorted to fabricated charges and kangaroo courts to convict Him. With a few words, He could have delivered Himself. He remained strangely quiet, for He had purposed to lay down His life for the sheep (John 10:15).

Our Shepherd knows about enemies, and He has already defeated every one of them. He laid down His life and He took it up again. And when He comes again, the song of the angels will be: "Alleluia! For the Lord God Omnipotent reigns!" (Revelation 19:6).

And He shall reign forever and ever (Revelation 11:15).

Our Lord Jesus Christ gives us the provisions of safety and victory on life's tableland. Because of Him, we can live on the heights without fear. He spreads a table for us in the presence of our enemies.

Our Shepherd gives joy unspeakable and full of glory,
and the fullness of power for service . . .
Abundant supply of every need . . .
life more abundantly.

—Dr. Robert C. McQuilkin[1]

9

His Potion for Life's Hurts

YOU ANOINT MY HEAD WITH OIL;
MY CUP RUNS OVER

My friend Duane Deckert, a pastor in Minot, North Dakota, is also a sheep rancher. He's raised livestock since his dad gave him a lamb to bottle-feed when he was a preschooler. Today he raises Hampshire sheep, and he recently told me that the parallel between shepherding and pastoring is uncanny.

"I really have two flocks," he said over lunch, "my sheep and my church, and it's eerie how similar they are. In fact, I sometimes look at a certain sheep in my flock and think of some particular member of my congregation. Sometimes the resemblance is unmistakable and even comical."

Duane has about seventy-five sheep now, but, oddly, he doesn't name them. He numbers his sheep. He can look at any particular sheep at any moment and know its number as well as he would know its name.

"I bought Number Twenty-seven some time ago," he said. "She's a ewe out of Ohio, and the first time she saw me, she ran to the back of the lot and wouldn't have anything to do with me. Normally sheep accept a new shepherd in a relatively short time because they learn the hand that feeds them. But Number Twenty-seven would have nothing to do with me for well over a year, maybe two years, after I bought her. She'd run to the back of the barn every time I'd come in.

"Then she hurt her foot," said Duane, "and I needed to tend her, but she wouldn't let me. She'd run away as fast as her sore foot would let her, and I could never catch her to help her. As a result, she limped for a long time.

"Then she got very sick, and there was no choice. I had to catch her and get her into a confined space so I could work with her. She needed very individual care with antibiotics and injections. As I doctored her, I talked to her. Gradually she warmed to me and began trusting me. During the process of tending and treating her in the stall, she finally accepted me as her shepherd. Now she's like any of the other sheep. Just the other day she was eating out of my hand. When I held the bucket out, she came right up to me. Number Twenty-seven has made an amazing transformation from a ewe that wanted nothing to do with me to one that has fully accepted me and allows me to care for her and her lambs."[2]

It's often during life's hurts that we come to understand the heart of the Shepherd, as we learn to accept His care and to trust His heart. As He tends us and mends us, we fall in love with Him and receive the comfort He gives. Troubles in life have a way of driving us to the Lord's tender mercies, and we bond with Him through the verses and vigor He bestows.

Psalm 23:5 speaks of the tending ministries of the Good

Shepherd when it says, "You anoint my head with oil; my cup runs over." The word *tend* is a wonderful biblical word—a shepherding term—that frequently occurs in Scripture. It comes from the Old English word *tenden,* from which we get our term *tendon.* It means "to stretch"; hence, we have its derivative words like *extend, attend,* and even *bartend.* It's the idea of stretching out the hand to do something. In the case of animal care, it's the shepherd's use of his extended hands to care for the individual needs of the sheep.

We first encounter this word in Genesis 2:15, when we're told that Adam and Eve were placed in the Garden of Eden "to *tend* and keep it." Presumably, that means tending to the animals as well as the plants that filled their paradisaical environment.

In Genesis 30, we're told that the patriarch Jacob was *tending* the flock of Laban. In Genesis 37, we see Joseph, a young man of seventeen, *tending* the flocks. Years later, after this young man had become a statesman and a ruler in Egypt, he described his family's business to his governmental colleagues, saying that they *tended* livestock (Genesis 46:32–33).

Exodus 3:1 says that Moses was *tending* the flocks of his father-in-law when God appeared to him in the burning bush.

Centuries later, when the prophet Samuel asked Jesse where his youngest son was, Jesse told him that David was *tending* the sheep.

In Luke 17, Jesus told a parable about a servant who was *tending* the sheep.

In John 21, the risen Christ met with the apostle Peter by the shores of Galilee and told him, "*Tend* my sheep."

The apostle Paul, suggesting that Christian workers have a

right to be supported financially, asked, "Who *tends* a flock and does not drink the milk of the flock?" (1 Corinthians 9:7). He told the Ephesian church leaders: "Keep watch over yourselves and over the whole flock of which the Holy Spirit has appointed you overseers, in which you *tend* the church of God that He acquired with His own blood" (Acts 20:28, NAB).

Tend is a tiny little four-letter word scattered throughout the Bible. It sums up so much of what shepherds do for their sheep and of what the Lord does for us. Two great passages of Scripture speak of this in visual terms.

- Isaiah 40:11 (NIV) says of our Lord: "He *tends* His flock like a shepherd: He gathers the lambs in His arms and carries them close to His heart; He gently leads those that have young."

- Ezekiel 34:11–16 (NIV 1984) says: "I Myself will search for My sheep and look after them. As a shepherd looks after his scattered flock when he is with them, so I will look after my sheep . . . I will pasture them on the mountains of Israel, in the ravines and in all the settlements in the land. I will *tend* them in a good pasture, and on the mountain heights of Israel will be their grazing land. There they will lie down in good grazing land, and there they will feed in a rich pasture on the mountains of Israel. I Myself will *tend* My sheep . . . I will bind up the injured and strengthen the weak."

Simply put, sheep require a lot of work, but the work is satisfying. I watched my girls tend their little flock of four or five sheep, and while it involved regular chores, it wasn't unpleasant for either the children or the sheep. The animals' hoofs had to be trimmed and cleaned out from time to time lest they became diseased and impacted. The sheep had to be wormed. Sometimes rotten teeth had to be extracted with pliers. Sheep need a mineral block lugged down the pasture and put near the water barrel, specifically one with very little copper, which sheep cannot tolerate. They had to be smeared with ointments to keep away the flies. Cuts and bruises needed to be washed and dressed.

The biggest job was shearing the sheep each spring. During the year, sheep grow heavy wool coats that keep them warm during the winter. It's remarkable how insulated those wool coats are. The wool is filled with lanolin, a waxy, waterproof substance secreted by glands in the sheep's skin. I always liked the way my hands felt after I'd handled the sheep, because lanolin is like a fine lotion.

Because of their warm and waterproof coats, our old sheep could lie down in the snow on a cold day and appear to be as comfortable as they were in springtime pastures. They seemed impervious to the cold, except on inclement nights when temperatures plunged to dangerous extremes. Then we'd round up our little flock and house them in the barn or basement.

There's only one problem with a sheep's overcoat: it won't do at all for summer. It's too heavy, too hot. All sheep need an annual haircut, but shearing a sheep is no easy task, either for the shepherd or for the flock. I always dreaded it, because of the sweaty work of rounding up a bunch of two-hundred-pound sheep, man-handling them onto their haunches, and trying to administer a shearing while they squirmed like two-year-olds.

A biblical character named Nabal didn't like sheep-shearing season either. In 1 Samuel 25, David showed up at Nabal's ranch wanting a handout. He couldn't have chosen a worse time. It was shearing season, and Nabal was in a foul mood. Without justifying Nabal's behavior, I do understand why he was rude and surly. He had three thousand sheep to shear, and in those days the job was done by hand with primitive tools. I would have been surly, too.

I always tried to hire out the job every year, but it's hard to get someone to come and barber a small number of sheep. Shearers get paid by the head, and they prefer going to ranches with large numbers of sheep. There's real money in that. But to drive all the way to our house to shear four or five old ewes—well, that was harder to arrange unless I could come up with a 4-H student wanting practice.

One year we had an early summer, and the temperatures peaked before our shearers could get to us. Fearing our flock would die from heat exhaustion, I went to the dime store and bought every pair of scissors on the shelves. We recruited our girls' friends and tackled the project. It was a pretty botched job, and when the shearer later came to finish the work, he laughed at us. But it got the job done. A good shearer can shave off the entire coat intact, which is valuable for its wool. My efforts at shearing left so many clumps of wool that they blew across the lawn like litter.

On one occasion, a farmer gave me a pair of discarded electric shears. They looked very much like the electric clippers used at barbershops, only much bigger and sturdier. I tried to shear the sheep by myself, but I wasn't really trained in the craft. It's easy to nick the sheep. They don't like to be sheared and are apt to squirm and jerk at the worst time. The shearer has to manhandle them, setting them on the haunches and trimming around delicate parts of their bodies. It's awfully easy to nip them in tender spots.

During the attempt, I learned why the farmer had given away the clippers. They kept giving me periodic shocks. Evidently, there was a short circuit in the system. It's too bad I don't have a video of the experience because it would be an internet sensation. I'd nick a sheep and she'd jump. A moment later, I'd get a little shock from the clippers and I'd jump. The neighbors must have thought we were having an old-time Gospel meeting, though it wasn't much of a revival for either the flock or me. The episode left me exhausted and the sheep felt, well, fleeced.

Which brings me to another point. We were always amused to watch the flock after they'd been sheared. The sheep were quite shy as they trotted back to the meadow, as if they felt naked. It also seemed to us that our sheep didn't recognize each other after they'd been shorn. They thought they were in a totally new flock and had to reestablish their "pecking order," so to speak. It takes sheep a day or two to recover from it all. Of course, as the days get hotter, they're glad to be in their summer attire.

In addition to tending to a sheep's physical needs, a good shepherd notices the emotional state of his flock. I think the most pitiful moment in our ranching experience was when we were down to two sheep, two old ewes, Lucy and Ethel. One day we looked out the window and Ethel was dead. She had just collapsed in the pasture and peacefully died of old age.

Lucy was standing beside her, looking skyward and bleating mournfully. She appeared as lost and as grief-stricken as a person who had lost her best friend. It broke our hearts. She wouldn't leave Ethel's side, and she clearly knew something terrible had happened and was grieving. We buried Ethel and didn't replace her. Our children were growing up and leaving home one by one, and Katrina's multiple sclerosis was worsening, so we reluctantly decided to phase out of the sheep-raising business. Lucy spent the next several years living alone in the pasture. Sheep are flock animals; they like companionship. They don't like to be alone. Lucy eventually managed to take up with the dog, and we all tried to go down to the field and fellowship with her each day. In time, just like a person, she seemed to adjust to her new realities.

Sheep are very much like human beings, and vice versa; they need a good shepherd to tend to them. We need a Great Shepherd to stay with us through all the experiences in life, someone to hover over us with an extended hand of mercy, someone to tend to us and our families and our needs.

In Psalm 23, David didn't list all the various duties he performed as a shepherd, but he did give us two items high on the list. He anointed his sheep with oil and made their troughs overflow.

You Anoint My Head with Oil

One day when I was checking on our sheep, I was alarmed to discover that the horse had evidently taken a serious bite out of Ethel's ear. A good portion of her ear had been torn away, and though I didn't see it happen, there was no other explanation except the horse, which was standing nearby trying his best to look innocent.

After pondering whether to call a vet, Psalm 23:5 came to mind. Grabbing a bottle of olive oil from the pantry, I washed Ethel's ear and rubbed that olive oil into the wound. It seemed to soothe her. After several treatments, the wound healed. Later as I was talking to a sheep exhibiter at the state fair about it, he said, "Oh, yes, that's a little trick we use at livestock shows. If we're showing a sheep and she gets a nick or a cut, we rub a little olive oil on it, and it does the trick."

The Good Shepherd is alert to various hurts, cuts, and problems we have. He anoints us with oil. Oil is a constant symbol in the Bible of the Holy Spirit and of the qualities that are Spirit-given, like joy and peace and patience (Galatians 5:22–23). The Lord knows how to heal our hurts and bind our wounds. He rubs the soothing oil onto the rough spots of life.

In the Bible, the words *Christ* and *Messiah* mean the "Anointed One." Our Lord Jesus was anointed with the oil of joy (Isaiah 61:3), of gladness (Psalm 45:7), of authority, power, wisdom, and understanding (Isaiah 11:2). He was anointed as prophet, priest, and king, which were all anointed offices (1 Kings 19:16; Exodus 28:41; 1 Samuel 16:13).

In Isaiah 61, we read of Him: "The Spirit of the Lord God is upon Me, because the Lord has anointed Me to preach good tidings . . . to heal . . . to proclaim liberty . . . to comfort . . . to give them beauty for ashes, the oil of joy for mourning, the garment of praise for the spirit of heaviness . . ."

When Jesus was baptized at the beginning of His ministry in the Gospels, the Holy Spirit descended on Him like a dove (Matthew 3:16) and anointed Him without measure or limit (John 3:34). That's why we call Jesus of Nazareth the "Christ." The Greek term *Christos* is a title that literally means "the Anointed One," and is the Greek rendition of the Hebrew term *Messiah*.

Here's the thrilling part. Just as our Great Shepherd was Himself anointed with the Spirit without measure, so He anoints His children with the spiritual oil of healing and gladness and power. He anoints us with the Holy Spirit, who has come to be with us and within us (John 14:17).

The ministry of the Holy Spirit pours on us all God's graces, and He infuses us with all-sufficient power. His presence abides with us. He is the Comforter, the Counselor, the One who comes alongside to help (John 14:16). The Holy Spirit makes real to us all the Father has planned for us and the Son provided for us. Christians are indwelled by the Holy Spirit and should walk in the Spirit (Galatians 5:16), be filled with the Spirit (Ephesians 5:18), be led by the Spirit (Galatians 5:18), display the graces of the Spirit (Romans 14:17), be empowered by the Spirit (Acts 4:31), and have the Holy Spirit within us as a deposit strengthening us and guaranteeing all God has for us in the future and in eternity (Romans 8:15–17 and 2 Corinthians 1:22).

Jill Briscoe talks about this in her delightful book *A Little Pot of Oil*. When she was six years old, she said, the German Luftwaffe bombarded Liverpool during the Battle of Britain. The docks were pounded night after night, forcing Jill's family and friends into the bomb shelters. One night in great fear she frantically tried to remember the Apostles' Creed, which was recited in her classroom at school. It began, "I believe in God the Father Almighty, Maker of heaven and earth." And then it goes on to say, ". . . and in Jesus Christ . . ." The explosions and the bombing were so intense that Jill repeated those words over and over to calm herself.

But when she got to the line "I believe in the Holy Ghost," she wondered who in the world that was. The last thing she wanted to think about in those dismal bomb shelters was a ghost, let alone a "holy" ghost. All in all, it was a disquieting thought to her, and that memory stayed with her for many years.

It was only after she became a Christian during her college days at Cambridge that she finally came back full circle to the question she had asked as a six-year-old girl in a Liverpool bomb shelter: Who is the Holy Ghost or the Holy Spirit?

"In the years following," wrote Jill Briscoe, "I have never stopped learning about the Spirit's sweet, abiding presence. He has drawn me to Christ as Savior and Lord and has ignited a passion in my soul for those who do not know Him. He has taught me how to pray when I didn't have a clue what to say, enlightened my mind to the Scriptures and thoroughly applied them to my life, and overwhelmed me with grace. He has strengthened me when I was weak, humbled me when I was proud, and sensitized me to sin. In fact, He has been all that I have needed Him to be, whenever I have needed Him."[3]

The Good Shepherd tends us by anointing us with the oil of His Spirit, and with the oil of the Spirit comes the anointing of joy, peace, healing, strength, and power.

My Cup Overflows

Another aspect of God's tending ministry is ensuring that we have plenty to drink even if we aren't near still ponds or quiet lakes. A good shepherd makes sure our watering troughs are full and overflowing. In describing the role of shepherds in the Old Testament, this was of utmost importance.

Genesis 29 tells us about the experience of Jacob along these lines: "Jacob went on his journey and came to the land of the people of the East. And he looked, and saw a well in the field; and behold, there were three flocks of sheep lying by it; for out of that well they watered the flocks. A large stone was on the well's mouth. Now all the flocks would be gathered there; and they would roll the stone from the well's mouth, water the sheep, and put the stone back in its place on the well's mouth."

Providing water for the sheep required a lot of work, especially on the tablelands away from natural rivers and ponds. A mature sheep needs between one and three gallons of water each day. Shepherds had to dig wells, and in biblical times, this was done by hand with crude shovels and picks. The wells had to be maintained, and a stone fitted for the covering. The wells had to be protected, and often were sources of bitter conflict between rival ranchers (Genesis 25:21–30). When time came to water the sheep, the stone was rolled away, buckets were dropped, and the water hauled up and poured into the troughs. The sheep didn't really appreciate all the work that went into it, but they were happy when their water troughs overflowed.

In Psalm 23, David was saying, "God's blessings have been poured out into my life so greatly that they overflow. I can't contain all of them. I can't absorb all the mercy and goodness that He has given me. I may not understand all it has cost My shepherd to provide such blessings, but I live in constant thanksgiving that my trough overflows. Goodness and mercy are certainly following me all the days of my life."

The Christian life is the overflowing life, and there's an important implication to that. As laborers in the Kingdom, our *work* for the Lord is simply the overflow of our *walk* with Him. Last year after I spoke at my alma mater, Columbia International University, a young man approached me with the kind of question I used to throw out to chapel speakers when I was a student there: "What one piece of advice would you give someone wanting to be in ministry?"

I answered instantly: "Always remember that ministry is overflow."

Too many of us drain the cup dry when trying to do the Lord's work, whereas true ministry is simply what flows over the rim. Jesus said, "For out of the overflow of the heart the mouth speaks" (Matthew 12:34, NIV).

If, for example, I go into the Bible as a preacher seeking sermons and looking for outlines, I'll find little more than a textbook to explain. But if I open the Bible to fellowship with my Lord and feed my own soul, the sermons and lessons will bubble over from within. If I try to help a needy person out of a sense of duty, I grow impatient; but if my good deeds are the overflow of the Christ-life within me, they'll be perennially fresh and fulfilling. To be vital in the Lord's work, we need to say with King David, "My cup runneth over."

In his memoir, *Just as I Am*, Billy Graham spoke of returning to his home in Montreat, North Carolina, in early 1954 in a state of fatigue. He was planning for an upcoming crusade in London, and he was nervous, tired, and worried. His wife, Ruth, gave him some counsel he never forgot:

> Ruth maintained in her counsel and advice to me that my studies should consist primarily of filling up spiritually. She believed, as I did, that God would give me the message and bring to remembrance in my preaching the things I had studied. This was always the most effective preaching, we had discovered: preaching that came from the overflow of a heart and mind filled not only with the Spirit but with much reading. Hence, I picked each sermon topic carefully, read myself full, wrote myself empty, and read myself full again on the subject.[4]

In John 4:14, Jesus promised that the water He gives us will become a spring of water welling up to eternal life. And in John

7:37, He took the analogy a step further, saying, "The one who believes in Me, as the Scripture has said, will have streams of living water flow from deep within him" (HCSB).

Whatever task the Lord gives us, we need to keep our hearts filled with the Spirit, and let the work be spillover. You'll find, like the widow of Zarephath in 1 Kings 17, that the jar of flour will not be used up and the jug of oil will not run dry.

The hymnist Frances Ridley Havergal prayed, "O fill me with Thy fullness, Lord, until my very heart overflow."[5]

Another nineteenth-century devotional writer, Hannah Whitall Smith, made a similar comment in her book, *The Christian's Secret of a Holy Life.* "My sister has had a glorious experience during her recent illness," she wrote. "She has entered into this life of abiding in Jesus, and is finding that it is a blessed life. She says . . . that she feels that she never before has known what it is to be buried with Christ and risen with Him to newness of life. She is just overflowing."[6]

Romans 15:13 (NIV) is perhaps the New Testament's best explanation of the overflowing cup of Psalm 23:5. The apostle Paul put it like this: "May the God of hope fill you with all joy and peace as you trust in Him, so that you may overflow with hope by the power of the Holy Spirit."

But, as I indicated earlier, while the sheep enjoy their overflowing cups, the cost to the shepherd is heavy. In Matthew 20, the twelve disciples were bickering among themselves about which ones should be in leadership. Upbraiding them, Jesus said, "You do not know what you ask. Are you able to drink the cup that I am about to drink?" He was referring to the cup of sorrow and pain He was soon to experience on the cross.

A few chapters later, we see Him in the Upper Room on the eve of His crucifixion. He again employs the symbolism of the cup. Matthew 26:27 says, "Then He took the cup, and gave thanks, and gave it to them, saying, 'Drink from it, all of you. For this is My blood of the new covenant, which is shed for many for the remission of sins.'"

The ruby-red wine in that small cup symbolized the vast ocean of God's crimson love poured out for us on the cross.

Later that evening in the Garden of Gethsemane, according to Matthew 26:39–45, Jesus fell with His face to the ground and prayed, "O My Father, if it is possible, let this cup pass from Me; nevertheless, not as I will, but as You will."

Moments later He prayed again, "O My Father, if this cup cannot pass away from Me unless I drink it, Your will be done."

Praying a third time, He repeated the same words, describing His suffering and death as a cup to be drained and drunk to the dregs.

Because Jesus drained His cup, ours can overflow. All our blessings in this life and the next—all were purchased for us by the Good Shepherd when He laid down His life for His sheep.

That's why it's so important to come to Christ and receive Him as Lord and Savior and to enter His fold and join His flock. He is a tending Shepherd. He prepares a table for us in the presence of our enemies, He anoints our heads with oil, and He so blesses our lives to overflowing that we can say with the old songwriter:

I shall not want: in deserts wild
Thou spread'st Thy table for Thy child;
While grace in streams for thirsting souls
Thro' earth and Heaven forever flows.[7]

May the Good Shepherd fill you with all joy and peace as you trust Him today, that your cup will overflow with the hope and power of the Holy Spirit!

Are we reading it,
"Goodness and mercy shall follow me
every now and then"?

—Dr. Robert C. McQuilkin[1]

10

His Promises
for Life's Journey

SURELY GOODNESS AND MERCY
SHALL FOLLOW ME ALL THE DAYS OF MY LIFE.

James Hogg (1770–1835) spent most of his youth herding flocks in rural Scotland and later published some of his popular novels under the pseudonym the Ettrick Shepherd. On one occasion, James recalled, he paid a guinea to buy a collie named Sirrah. The dog had good herding instincts, and the young man began training him to tend the flock. Sirrah was highly intelligent, and he seemed to try to figure out what James wanted him to do. After learning a trick or technique, the dog never forgot it. Sirrah also had enough native instinct to invent ways of overcoming obstacles and getting out of difficulties.

One afternoon about seven hundred lambs were moved to a certain pasture. It was their first evening away from their mothers, and they were jittery and fretful. It was a very dark night, and something happened that panicked the animals. They seemed to separate into three groups that bolted into the darkness in three directions. James and his helper tried to stop them, but it was no use.

"Sirrah! They're away!" cried the boys. The dog took off like a bullet into the night and wasn't seen again. The young men, having lost both their lambs and their dog, spent the whole night traversing the mountains and meadows, searching and calling for the missing animals. But inky darkness seemed to have swallowed everything like a bottomless pit.

As the sun rose, the boys had no choice but to report the loss to the farmer who owned the flock. James later said it was an appalling confession, for no one in those parts had ever heard of losing seven hundred sheep in a single night or of having one's flocks vanish into thin air. After delivering the news, he wearily trudged toward home. Along the way, James passed a deep hollow. To his astonishment, there below him were all seven hundred lambs. They were grazing contentedly at the bottom of the valley with Sirrah standing guard over them. At first, James thought the dog must have rounded up just one of the three groups of AWOL sheep, but when he lined up and counted the lambs, all seven hundred were there. Not one was missing.

"How Sirrah had managed to collect them nobody knew," he later wrote, "and of course nobody ever *did* know."[2]

I believe this story can help us understand Psalm 23:6. Toward the end of the Twenty-third Psalm, David's thoughts go to the dogs, so to speak. Sheep aren't the only animals in this poem; there are sheepdogs as well. We can base this insight on the Hebrew verb *follow,* as David writes, "Surely goodness and mercy shall *follow* me."

"Follow" is a feeble translation of the Hebrew word *rapad,* which is found more than 150 times in the Old Testament. It's usually translated "pursued," "chased," or "hunted." As we encounter this word in Scripture, it typically describes being pursued by an enemy or by an animal. David used this word in 1 Samuel 26:20, when he said the armies of Saul were pursuing him "as when one *hunts* a partridge in the mountains."

Here in Psalm 23:6, David used the same Hebrew word to refer to his being pursued by *goodness* and *mercy,* and commentators have long speculated that David's use of the verb indicated that he was thinking of his herding dogs. In rural lands, you'll often see the shepherd going in front of the flock leading the way, followed by all the sheep, with sheepdogs bringing up the rear and running along the sides of the flock to keep them from straggling or straying.

Although the nature of the Hebrew verb is my only justification for extrapolating "dogs" out of verse 6, and it may not be the most conclusive exegetical evidence, I find it to be an inspiring application.

It's fascinating to read about herding dogs. They're found all over the world in every kind of agricultural society, and they're trained to act on the sound of a word or a whistle. Sheepdogs keep the livestock on the trail and move them one way or the other in traveling, using their barks and aggressive movements to help corral and control the flock. Sometimes they nip at the sheep, running back and forth and from side to side, chasing after strays, snapping at them and keeping the flock together.

Storey's Guide to Raising Sheep, a standard textbook for sheep ranchers, devotes an entire chapter to the subject of herding dogs. The authors write:

> A well-trained stock dog can be an enormous help to you as a shepherd. It can greatly reduce the amount of equipment required for sheep handling. The dog can drive stock from one pasture to another, load one sheep (or hundreds) into corrals or stock trailers, or work with you as you operate a squeeze chute for pregnancy checking, shearing, or worming. A good dog can single out one animal without moving the entire flock to a sorting facility. During lambing, it can help bring in expectant mothers . . . And you will truly know the value of a herding dog when it comes to escaped sheep—it regathers them easily, whereas without a dog you could have serious trouble capturing the wayward sheep. In short, a good stock dog can be of more help than several human helpers.[3]

The best sheepdogs can control the flock with their eyes, and sheep ranchers regularly talk about dogs "with eye" and dogs "without eye." A dog with a good "eye" can stare down the flock without so much as a growl.

In Europe, it's not uncommon to see flocks that are chiefly kept by a dog. A nearby caretaker may keep a casual eye on the flock, but it's the dog that takes the sheep out to graze each morning, patrols along the parameters of the grazing area, sounds the alarm if a predator appears in the area, and herds them back to the fold at the end of day. Furthermore, they're cheap labor: will work for food.

And that brings up another function of dogs. If necessary, they'll protect the flock. Many shepherds have two sets of dogs—herding dogs and guardian dogs. But sometimes the same dog must assume both duties. Dogs, with their keen hearing and acute sense of smell, can detect a threatening presence long before the shepherd does.

This might be a good time to lay aside this book and watch a sheepdog training video or a film from a competitive herding trial. You can find them easily on the internet. Competitive herding competitions are popular around the world, and some of the events even show up on prime-time television. It's remarkable to watch the dogs perform. The best of them herd with effortless efficiency. They're as skilled as professional athletes, yet they seem to enjoy themselves like youngsters playing soccer.

Not surprisingly, an entire vocabulary has arisen along these lines. If the handler shouts, "Come-bye," the dog knows to circle the flock in a clockwise direction. "Way-to-me" instructs the dog to circle in a counterclockwise direction. "Down" means to stop the flock in their tracks, and "Steady" means to slow down. "Walk up" signals the dog to move toward the sheep, and "Look back" tells him to leave the primary flock to chase down a stray or look for another group of sheep nearby. When the dog hears the words "That'll do," he knows to stop working; he's now off the clock.[4]

For the relationship to work, dogs and sheep must bond. Despite its energy and aggressive demeanor, a good stock dog will love its flocks and protect them at all costs. It's a reassuring and vital relationship that satisfies all three parties—dogs, sheep, and shepherd.

In her book *This Was Sheep Ranching Yesterday and Today,* Virginia Paul told about a large herd being kept on a remote mountain range in Oregon. Supplies were shipped into the herder every other week. At some point during the interval, the shepherd died of natural causes. On his next periodic visit, the supplier found the shepherd dead but the sheep still well cared for. Their canine shepherd herded them out every morning and into the fold every evening. Under his watchful eye, not a single sheep was missing.

"Furthermore," added Paul, "the dog had been traveling several miles each day to another sheep camp where he was given some biscuits. The biscuits were not eaten but were brought back and placed by the herder's body. The dog had done his best to provide food for his friend and master."[5]

We know that Turkish shepherds migrated with their sheep and dogs in the thirteenth century and that sheep ranchers in Italy used guard dogs with their flocks as far back as we can study. Herding dogs have pushed flocks across Great Britain from Neolithic times. I consider it a virtual certainty that David used dogs to tend his sheep, and I think that's why he used this vigorous term *rapad* in Psalm 23:6. He was expanding the analogy of the poem, telling us that the Good Shepherd who goes before us has twin sheepdogs named "Goodness" and "Mercy" who follow us, nipping at our heels. "Goodness" scampers beside us with boundless energy, making sure we're surrounded with God's protective and proactive care. "Mercy" runs along behind, guarding our rear flanks, nipping at us if we lag, and retrieving us if we lose our way.

Surely

With that as our basic insight, let's go back to the beginning of the verse. The first word is *surely*: "Surely goodness and mercy shall chase me." When I memorized Psalm 23 in grade school, I misunderstood that phrase. For years, I childishly thought it represented a string of three things that were following me: surely, mercy, and goodness.

The original Hebrew term that David used is a very small word that can mean either "surely" or "only." Some translations say, "Only goodness and mercy." But the best rendering seems to be "surely." It has the basic meaning of "no doubt; this is absolutely true; this can never be doubted; it can never fail."

Those of us who grew up reading the King James Version of the Bible remember the "verily" statements of Christ: "Verily, verily, I say unto you . . ." This phrase conveyed the same idea. Jesus was saying, "I'm going to tell you something that is very true, highly certain, eternally established, and totally factual."

The Bible is full of terminology that conveys the confidence we should have in our Lord and His Word. The apostle Paul said, "I am persuaded that neither death nor life, nor angels nor principalities nor powers, nor things present nor things to come, nor height or depth, nor any other created things, shall be able to separate us from the love of God which is in Christ Jesus our Lord" (Romans 8:38–39).

The patriarch Job said, "I know that my Redeemer lives" (Job 19:25).

In 2 Corinthians, the apostle Paul said, ". . . having confidence . . . so we are always confident . . . We are confident . . . I have confidence . . . because of the great confidence which we have . . ." (2:3, 5:6, 5:8, 7:16, 8:22).

The apostle John said, "These things I have written to you . . . that you may know . . . This is the confidence we have . . ." (1 John 5:13–14).

We're told that Abraham was "fully convinced that what [God] had promised He was also able to perform" (Romans 4:21 KJV).

The apostle Peter said, "Now I know for certain . . ." (Acts 12:11).

Persuaded, convinced, know, confident, certain—surely!

This is why the Lord is grieved when we don't trust Him. When anxiety steals our peace, and worry erodes our mind; it's a sign that we're forgetting the force of this adverb in Psalm 23:6: *Surely* . . . Here is something that must never be doubted. Here are two sheepdogs who never go off duty.

Goodness and Mercy Shall Follow Me

Goodness is almost too big a biblical term to describe. The Hebrew word David used refers to goodness in its broadest sense, covering physical, moral, practical, economic, spiritual, emotional, and eternal grace toward us in all its dimensions. The word *good* is a characteristic of God, and it refers to the essential nature of His perfections and benevolence. He is a good God, and He continually fills our lives with goodness and with good things. Jesus referred to Himself as the "Good Shepherd" who gives His sheep abundant life (John 10:10).

One of my favorite techniques of Bible study is investigating a verse by looking up its cross-references. Whenever we read a verse, we encounter words or phrases that are found elsewhere in the Bible, and we come across themes that are mentioned in other Bible verses. As we trace these cross-references, our insights are expanded. Often a good study Bible will have a column of such cross-references in the margin of every page. Or you can utilize a resource such as *The New Treasury of Scripture Knowledge* that lists multiple cross-references for virtually every verse in the Bible.

When we track down the cross-references to the phrase "goodness . . . shall follow me all the days of my life," we have more than we can list. For example, Psalm 100 says, "We are His people and the sheep of His pasture . . . Be thankful to Him, and bless His name. For the Lord is good."

Psalm 21:3 says, "You meet [me] with the blessings of goodness."

Psalm 34:10 says, "Those who seek the Lord shall not lack any good thing."

Psalm 84:11 adds, "No good thing will He withhold from those who walk uprightly."

Jesus said, "If you then, being evil, know how to give good gifts to your children, how much more will your Father who is in heaven give good things to those who ask Him!" (Matthew 7:11).

James said, "Every good and perfect gift is from above, and comes down from the Father of lights" (James 1:17).

The Bible says, "From the fullness of His grace we have all received one blessing after another" (John 1:16, NIV 1984). And so we say: "Praise be to the God and Father of our Lord Jesus Christ, who has blessed us in the heavenly realms with every spiritual blessing in Christ" (Ephesians 1:3, NIV 1984).

This theme in the Bible has literally changed my personality. I'm aware that many psychologists tell us we can't really change our temperaments. According to modern thinking, we're born with biologically predetermined personalities and preset temperaments, and there's not a lot we can do to alter them. But I don't believe it. I'm melancholy by nature, and if I let myself, I could drift into depression like a swimmer being pulled out to sea. But by God's grace and along with many other Christian believers, I'm learning how to live joyfully by claiming the Bible verses of God's goodness toward me, His blessings to me, and the biblical reassurances of His grace in all its dimensions. He transforms us from the inside out as we discover that the joy of the Lord is the strength of our lives.

If you're struggling to maintain your good attitudes or upbeat spirit, concentrate your attention on some of the verses listed above. Memorize them. Visualize them. Personalize them. Recognize that Psalm 23:6 wants us to be convinced that God's goodness is herding us like a faithful sheepdog every single day of our lives.

Dr. Robert McQuilkin, from whose little booklet on the Twenty-third Psalm I've taken the quotes for the chapter headings, once observed that the difference between victory and defeat is the position of the word *but*. We tend to say, "The Lord is my shepherd, but . . ."

I can't pay my bills.

I don't feel well.

I'm worried about this problem.

We should say, "I'm presently having trouble paying my bills, but the Lord is my Shepherd. I may not feel well, but the Lord is my Shepherd. His goodness follows me all the days of my life."

"The testimony of victory puts the *but* into the right place," wrote McQuilkin.[6]

Where would we be *but* for His goodness?

And not just His goodness, but His mercy. The word *mercy* means kindness. This is the great Old Testament word for the loyal and royal love of God. The Old Testament phrase "goodness and mercy" corresponds to the New Testament benedictions of "grace and mercy" frequently mentioned in the apostolic letters as a blessing.

It's in God's nature to be merciful, forgiving, and benevolent. He surrounds our lives with acts of grace we could never earn by our own efforts, all because of His loyal and steadfast love for us. Goodness represents all He bestows on us that we *don't* deserve. Mercy represents all He withholds that we *do* deserve.

All the Days of My Life

The final phrase in the first line of Psalm 23:6 gives us the duration of God's goodness and mercy. They extend to every day and to all our days. There are no "blackout days" to worry about: no exclusions, no exceptions, no exemptions. His sheepdogs never take a day off, and they remain awake every night.

Here in the last verse of Psalm 23, we encounter the future tense for the first time. The writer says: "Goodness and mercy *shall* follow me"—and that makes verse 6 a promise, not just a statement of fact. We're now in promise territory where future assurances are given. Promiseland is the richest pasturage in Scripture. This verse is a promise—*shall*—that God's goodness and mercy will surround us every day from now until He takes us home to heaven.

This verse also provides one of the Bible's great "all"s. Some years ago, I went through the Bible looking up every reference to the word *all,* a study that's published in my devotional book *All to Jesus.* In the introduction of that work, I wrote that *all* is

> . . . one of God's favorite words. He used it thousands of times, often in passages that would have read nicely without it; yet the *all* maximizes the meaning to the absolute. It's the largest little word in the world, taking already-strong statements and broadening their applications to virtual infinity, which, after all, is what one would expect from an omnipotent Father.
>
> The frequency of this word in Scripture speaks

to the all-sufficient grace of our Almighty Savior. It highlights the infinite omni-qualities of God, and the complete devotion we should afford Him. He is the Lord of All, our All-in-All, our Almighty God, our All-Sufficient Savior from whom All blessings flow; and He is All we need.

Looking up all these *all*s was the simplest Bible study I've ever done, but one of the most bolstering to the soul, because all Scripture is given by inspiration of God—even the thousands of occurrences of this little monosyllabic term.[7]

We're told that *all* things work together for good, that the hairs of our head have *all* been numbered, that if we seek first His kingdom, *all* these things will be added to us, that He is faithful and just to forgive *all* our unrighteousness, that we can cast *all* our cares on Him, and that goodness and mercy follow *us* all the days of our lives (Romans 8:28, Matthew 10:30, Matthew 6:33, 1 John 1:9, 1 Peter 5:7, Psalm 23:6).

This doesn't mean we won't face adversity or have any dark days, because the psalmist has already warned us that our pathway may wind through dark valleys. But it does promise that *every day* for the Christian will be filled with God's mercy and goodness. Neither the Shepherd nor His twin sheepdogs will forget us or forsake us.

The prophet Jeremiah said, "His compassions never fail. They are new every morning; great is Your faithfulness" (Lamentations 3:22–23, NIV 1984).

Psalm 25:10 says, "All the paths of the Lord are mercy and truth, to such as keep His covenant and His testimonies." And Psalm 103:17 adds, "The mercy of the Lord is from everlasting to everlasting on those who fear Him, and His righteousness to children's children."

We're a blessed flock! As the renowned British poet George Herbert put it in his classic poem, "The Temple":

> *Surely Thy sweet and wondrous love*
> *Shall measure all my days;*
> *And as it never shall remove,*
> *So neither shall my praise.*

When a believer dies, his spirit is so instantaneously
in the presence of the Lord that he may feel with Paul
that he knows not whether he is in the body
or out of the body (2 Corinthians 12:1–4).

—Dr. Robert C. McQuilkin[1]

His Palaces at Life's End

AND I WILL DWELL
IN THE HOUSE OF THE LORD FOREVER.

$\mathcal{T}$he genius of Psalm 23 is its simplicity. We're all longing for the simple life. Everyone wants to escape the dizzying spin of complexity and confusion and to rectify our out-of-control world. Well, nothing is simpler than Psalm 23, as we see in this condensed version:

- Beside Me: My Shepherd

- Beneath Me: Green Pastures

- Near Me: Still Waters

- Ahead of Me: Righteous Paths

- Within Me: Restored Spirits

- Against Me: My Enemies

- For Me: His Rod and Staff

- Around Me: A Tableland

- Upon Me: Anointing Oil

- Above Me: Overflowing Blessings

- Behind Me: Goodness and Mercy

- Before Me: My Father's House

As we finish our study of Psalm 23, we're coming full circle at the end of the season and coming to that last reality—Before Me: My Father's House. We started in the springtime pastures of Hebron and Bethlehem. As spring merged with summer, we headed north, hiking from pasture to pasture, going onward and upward. Our trails sometimes wound through difficult canyons and wild gorges. We've enjoyed the highlands of Galilee with their sloping pastures and overflowing troughs. And now the season is nearly over, winter is at hand, and we are heading home.

With its final line, Psalm 23 comes full circle, back to the Father's House: "I shall dwell in the house of the Lord forever." For David's literal flocks in biblical times, the trail spiraled back to Hebron and Bethlehem as they returned to the family farm at the end of their seasonal migrations. For believers, our trail spirals upward as we arrive at our Father's House at the end of our earthly road. Here in Psalm 23:6, David is thinking of heaven, which he describes as "the house of the Lord."

The House of the Lord

The phrase "the house of the Lord" occurs many times in the Old Testament, and we can learn a lot by checking the cross-references. It frequently appears in other psalms. Just four psalms up the street from Psalm 23, for example, is Psalm 27, in which David said: "One thing I have desired of the Lord, that will I seek: That I may dwell in *the house of the Lord* all the days of my life, to behold the beauty of the Lord, and to inquire in His temple" (v. 4, emphasis mine here and in the following verses).

Psalm 92 says, "The righteous shall flourish like a palm tree, He shall grow like a cedar in Lebanon. Those who are planted *in the house of the Lord* shall flourish in the courts of our God" (v. 12–13).

Psalm 122 says, "I was glad when they said unto me, 'Let us go into *the house of the Lord*'" (v. 1, KJV).

In the Old Testament, *the house of the Lord* was the Tabernacle and later the Temple. It was the place where God dwelled among His people. The first time we see this phrase in the Bible is in Exodus 23:19, when the Lord told the Children of Israel, "The first of the first fruits of your land you shall bring into *the house of the Lord* your God."

In 1 Samuel, when Hannah and her family wanted to join in the great worship convocations of Israel, they went up to Shiloh to *the house of the Lord*; when Samuel was born, she brought him to *the house of the Lord* and left him there to be mentored by the old priest Eli (1 Samuel 1:7 and 24). This was the location of the

Tabernacle, which represented the localized presence of the omnipresent God among His people.

As we read through the Old Testament, we're told that Solomon built the Temple as *the house of the Lord* in Jerusalem (1 Kings 7:51), and when it was dedicated, the Lord descended in such clouds of glory that "the priests could not continue ministering because of the cloud; for the glory of the Lord filled *the house of the Lord*" (1 Kings 8:11).

The house of the Lord is the place where God's presence is centered. It represents the place of His throne, the place where He lives in the immediate essence of His presence. In short, the house of the Lord is the presence of the Lord. David was saying, "I will live in the presence of the Lord." And his final word—*forever*—lets us know he was thinking of heaven, to the city of New Jerusalem, where "the tabernacle [house] of God is with men, and He will dwell with them, and they shall be His people. God Himself will be with them and be their God" (Revelation 21:3).

On the eve of His crucifixion, Jesus spoke of this in His "Upper Room Discourse," recorded for us verbatim in John 13–17. Referring to Psalm 23:6 and to the prospect about living in *the house of the Lord* forever, our Lord said, "Let not your heart be troubled; you believe in God, believe also in Me. In *My Father's house* are many mansions; if it were not so, I would have told you. I go to prepare a place for you. And if I go and prepare a place for you, I will come again and receive you to Myself; that where I am, there you may be also" (John 14:1–3).

The Father's House is Heaven, where we will enjoy His presence forever and live in the mansions Jesus is preparing for us—His palaces at life's end.

I memorized John 14:1–6 about the same time I memorized Psalm 23, in the early elementary years. The two passages go together like hand in glove. I learned both passages in the old King James Version, where the word *mansions* appeared without qualification. Newer translations tend to downplay the word, saying, "In My Father's house are many rooms or chambers or dwelling places."

I'm sticking with "mansions" on the assumption that the smallest hut in heaven will be a thousand times greater than any house that's ever been built on earth. Many of us have occasionally imagined what it'd be like to live in a mansion. Maybe you've toured castles or palaces or regal estates. Haven't you wondered what it'd be like to throw open the door and holler, "Honey, I'm home!" Perhaps you've driven by exclusive communities or looked at magazine photographs of celebrities' homes. Once when we were vacationing with our girls in California, Katrina and I bought a map of the "Homes of the Stars" and spent a delightful afternoon driving around Hollywood seeing where everyone lived.

None of the homes came close to the homesteads Jesus is preparing for us in heaven. Of course, I have no idea about the square footage of our heavenly abodes, but Jesus did say, "In My Father's house are many mansions; if it were not so, I would have told you." And the next day, He told the dying thief on the cross, "Today you will be with Me in paradise" (Luke 23:43). The word *paradise* has its roots in the Persian language. It was used to describe a beautiful garden, usually enclosed within stone walls, that was well cultivated, spreading, verdant, and typically set aside as a private park for the royal family. A place of paradise was one of privacy, lush cultivation, absolute security, and breathtaking beauty.

Jesus was indicating to the dying thief that the two of them would be in heaven—the Father's House with its mansions, paradise with its marvels—before the sun went down on earth. Later the apostle Paul spoke of being caught up into paradise where he heard inexpressible words (2 Corinthians 12:4). John also used this word in Revelation 2:7, when he talked about "the tree of life, which is in the midst of the paradise of God."

The New Heavens and the New Earth

Over the years, I've had the opportunity of visiting some of the most beautiful spots on earth. I've seen the Grand Canyon of Arizona and the Copper Canyon of Mexico. I've seen the mighty Iguaçu Falls of Brazil and the towering Alps of Austria. I've been to the Arctic Circle of Finland and to the Great Wall of China. I've flown over the vast wastelands of the Sahara in North Africa and walked across the White Sands of New Mexico. I've hiked into Petra, bicycled along the Danube, driven along the French Riviera, hiked through Italian fishing villages, and snorkeled in the Caribbean. In trying to take in the majesty of these vistas, I've often thought of the old Gospel song that says, "How beautiful heaven must be!"

If this sin-filled, pollution-spoiled world is so beautiful now, can you imagine the pristine beauty that will surround us throughout eternity in the Father's house? In paradise? There will be beauty without measure on the New Earth.

A couple of years ago I was flying out of New York City at dusk, and I happened to be on the side of the airplane that had the million-dollar view of Manhattan at twilight. On the lower end was the Statue of Liberty, midway up was the Empire State Building, and on up farther was Central Park, and all the millions of glittering lights from a thousand skyscrapers. It was breathtaking.

But it's nothing compared to the city John saw in Revelation 21 and 22. In these final chapters of the Bible, we learn that at the end of the age, God is going to literally melt down the universe and remake it into a new universe, new stars, new galaxies, and new planetary systems. He's going to make a New Earth, surrounded by New Heavens.

The New Heavens and New Earth will be literal, physical, pristine, sinless, and beautiful. Descending onto the New Earth will be the City of New Jerusalem, glittering like an enormous jewel, translucent and luminescent in its beauty. In Revelation 21 and 22, the apostle John is given a tour of the City with foundations whose building and maker is God.

- In the first part of chapter 21, John begins with an overarching summary of the New Heavens and the New Earth, then zeroes in on what this great city will look like as it descends to this earth like a gigantic diamond.

- In the middle of Revelation 21, John surveys the walls, gates, and foundations. We see the city from the exterior.

- In the last part of chapter 21, we slip through one of the gates right into the city itself. The first thing John noticed is what is absent—there is no temple, no need for the sun or the moon, no shut gates, no night, and no sin.

- In the first part of chapter 22, we travel to the City Center when we find the Throne of God, the central golden boulevard of the city, the Crystal River, and Tree of Life Park.

I view all those descriptions as literal realities. Jesus rose from the dead with a literal and physical body, glorified for eternity. He ate with the disciples. They touched Him. The risen Christ wasn't a disembodied spirit but a truly resurrected and glorified person, equipped to dwell in a physical environment. I believe the Father's house is real, paradise is tangible, and the New Heavens and the New Earth are literal realities.

Hebrews 11:13–16 says about the heroes of the Bible: "[They] confessed that they were strangers and pilgrims on the earth . . . They seek a homeland . . . They desire a better, that is, a heavenly country. Therefore God is not ashamed to be called their God, for He has prepared a city for them."

"Here we have no continuing city," adds Hebrews 13:14, "but we seek the one to come."

Some time ago, I spoke at a church in Portsmouth, Ohio, and as I was getting in my car to leave, a couple came up to me. Don and Mae Cregger are elderly but energetic and cheerful. They very much wanted to tell me something before I drove off.

The Creggers have a daughter who is a nurse, and some time ago, when Mrs. Cregger began suffering from what appeared to be severe heartburn, this daughter suggested they visit the hospital. At the hospital, the doctor who examined Mrs. Cregger became concerned. He detected a heart problem. Mrs. Cregger was sent by ambulance to a larger hospital for treatment. There doctors found five serious blockages in her heart, and she was taken into the operating room for surgery.

After the surgery, Mr. Cregger and the daughter were with her in the recovery room when everything went wrong. The heart monitor flatlined, the daughter screamed, and medical personnel leaped into action, trying to save the woman's life. Both the daughter and the husband had a strong sense that the woman had died, and they seemed to feel her soul leaving her body. They were ushered out of the room as the medical experts tended the dying woman and managed to get her heart beating again. It was such a strange sensation that the father and daughter agreed to say nothing about it. "Let's not tell anyone about this," advised Mr. Cregger.

Mae was never told how close she had come to dying. Later, after she had recovered enough to be released, everyone was home preparing supper. As they talked, Mrs. Cregger said in an almost casual way that she "must have died" in the hospital. Father and daughter looked at each other and asked her why she would say that.

"Well," she said, "I remember feeling my spirit leave my body. I was propelled toward a wondrous light at the end of a pathway. It was a propulsion pushing me onward, but not at all unpleasant. I was traveling down a lovely pathway, unfamiliar but pleasant, with flowers blooming on both sides, everywhere. They were beautiful, but I didn't recognize the varieties. I also heard music, and it was beautiful, but I didn't recognize the songs. At the end of the pathway in front of me, a man in white was beckoning for me to come. But then suddenly he stopped and held up his hands and motioned for me to go back. And that's when I guess I revived in the recovery room."

I asked Mrs. Cregger if the experience had made her feel differently about death, and she replied matter-of-factly, "Well, I guess; but I've never been afraid of death to begin with. I'm looking forward to being with the Lord."

We never build our theology or establish our beliefs on the basis of personal experiences or testimonies. We base our doctrine solely on the Bible. Nonetheless, I find it encouraging to read or hear the stories of countless Christians throughout history who have apparently glimpsed the outskirts of heaven while at death's door.

Even without these testimonies, however, we're assured of the wonders of dwelling in the house of the Lord forever. Several months ago, I conducted a worship service at a retirement home in Nashville. Afterward, an aged woman pulled me aside. She and her husband, she told me, had been married more than sixty years. During their final years together, they used my book *Then Sings My Soul* for their morning devotions. This is a devotional book of hymn stories, and every morning the couple read the story about the hymn and then sang the song. One morning they came to the old song that was very popular in its day (and is still a favorite of mine). Written by Charles Gabriel, it was commonly called "The Glory Song." The words say:

> *When all my labors and trials are o'er*
> *And I am safe on that beautiful shore,*
> *Just to be near the sweet Lord I adore*
> *Will thro' the ages be glory for me.*

> *O that will be glory for me*
> *Glory for me, glory for me.*
> *When by His grace I shall look on His face,*
> *That will be glory, be glory for me.*

The husband read that song and the story about it, and he said to his wife, "That will be glory for me. I'm ready to go right now."

"But what about me?" she asked.

"Oh," he said, "you have a lot of people to look after you. When I get to heaven, that will be glory for me."

Later that very day, she told me, he keeled over and died. The Lord took him to his heavenly home. It was unexpected, but the memory of that final serious conversation comforted the woman in a way that gave her perfect peace and inner joy.

Verse 3 of that old hymn says:

> *Friends will be there I have loved long ago,*
> *Joy like a river around me will flow;*
> *Yet just a smile from my Savior I know,*
> *Will through the ages be glory for me.*

Never forget that the last word of Psalm 23 is the first word of eternity.

We're traveling under the watchful eye of the "Great Shepherd of the Sheep." He knows us by name, carries us in His heart, and leads us on our circuit through life's pastures and passages. We wander from still waters to stormy climes. We're sometimes surrounded by breathtaking beauty and sometimes encompassed by bloodthirsty foes. We're often bewildered and sometimes cast down. But in truth we have everything we need, and our Shepherd is never in the least rattled or lost.

He knows the way home.

We shall dwell in the house of the Lord—forever!

CONCLUSION

The Shepherd Is My Lord!

In my hometown of Elizabethton, Tennessee, lived an aged schoolteacher named Beula Thomas, a friend of my mother's, who was raised on the Colorado prairie. Before her death, Beula recorded her childhood recollections, including the vivid incident that brought her to faith in Jesus Christ.

An early blizzard hit the Rockies during the winter of 1912, and a local shepherd, Mr. Woods, was caught with his flock in the mountains near the Thomas homestead. He desperately tried to herd his sheep into a hollow space close together so they could keep warm. Woods knew the thick snow would provide a protective covering for his sheep, saving them from the bitter wind, and the respiration of the sheep would melt the snow near their faces, allowing them to breathe.

But instead of following their shepherd, the sheep bolted after the lead sheep and ran into a thick snowdrift, where they perished. The despondent, half-frozen shepherd showed up at the Thomas house seeking refuge from the storm. Mrs. Thomas heated water for the poor man's hands and feet while her husband rubbed them vigorously to ward off frostbite. Over a supper of salmon patties, the man told his sad story. "I'll come back after the blizzard and skin the sheep," said Mr. Woods. "The birds and coyotes will take care of the meat." The three Thomas children were gripped by this unexpected visitor and his story.

Shortly afterward, as they discussed it all with their mother, she quoted Psalm 23, explaining that Jesus is the Good Shepherd who cares for us, though we all like sheep have gone astray. "Some people are stubborn and refuse to follow Christ and are lost forever. But Jesus came to lead his sheep to eternal safety." As she used that story to explain the Gospel, her words spoke to the children, and that day both Beula and sister Pearl chose to follow the Master's voice.

I hope you know the Lord Jesus Christ, too, and that you've chosen to follow Him as your Shepherd.

Jesus applied Psalm 23 to Himself in John, chapter 10, but He didn't do it the way we do. When we read Psalm 23, we think of ourselves as the sheep. When Jesus read this, He thought of Himself as the Shepherd. He said, "I am the good Shepherd, and I lay down My life for My sheep."

Every verse of Psalm 23, every phrase, every promise, every image, every word was purchased and paid for by the blood of Jesus Christ. And the Bible tells us we must confess Him as Lord and know in our hearts that He died and rose again for us.

Here are two ways of putting Psalm 23 into practice.

First, make this your psalm. In his book *God's Psychiatry,* Dr. Charles L. Allen told of a man who came to see him. This fellow had risen to the top of his company, but along the way he had lost his peace of mind. He was a worried, tense, sick man. He'd been to doctors and taken bottles of pills, but nothing helped.

Dr. Allen took out a sheet of paper and wrote a "prescription" for the man. He prescribed the Twenty-third Psalm five times a day for seven days. He insisted the man carry out the assignment to the letter. Upon awakening each morning, the man was to read through the psalm carefully, meditatively, and prayerfully. Immediately after breakfast, he was to do the same, then after lunch, again after dinner, and finally the last thing before going to bed.

Allen gave the prescription with the confidence that it would work, because he had given out that same advice many times, and it had never failed. "That prescription sounds simple," he wrote in his book, "but really it isn't. The Twenty-third Psalm is one of the most powerful pieces of writing in existence, and it can do marvelous things for any person. I have suggested this to many people, and in every instance where I know it was tried, it always produced results. It can change your life in seven days."[1]

Try it for yourself and make Psalm 23 your psalm.

Second, make the Good Shepherd your Shepherd. You can't say, "The Lord is my Shepherd" unless you also say, "The Shepherd is my Lord." The Lordship of Christ is the willingness to follow the Shepherd wherever He goes, as the old hymn says: "His faithful follower I would be, for by His hand He leadeth me." It takes commitment, brings contentment, and takes us on an adventure retracing the route that leads from our home below to our home above.

The journey starts wherever you are. My friend Clint Morgan, who travels the world for global missions, told me of a young man he met in Tajikistan who was assigned to work in a notorious prison near the city of Kudjand, but he got off to a rough start. Arriving at the prison, he was escorted to a dark room occupied by an old murderer sitting cross-legged on the floor.

"What do you want, boy?" snarled the hardened man.

The young fellow was so unnerved that he dropped his Bible. As he picked it up, it opened to Psalm 23, which he proceeded to try to read. The old man responded by taunting him, "What are you going to do, boy, try to turn us all into sheep?"

"No," stammered the worker, "I just want to tell you how to find green pastures." He returned home with a stabbing sense of failure but returned the next week. This time he walked into the room to find it packed with prisoners. In the middle of them sat the murderer. He said, "Son, we want you to tell us how to find the green pastures."

As best he could, the worker shared the message of the Good Shepherd. As he finished, the elderly convict said, "Young man, I want to go to those green pastures"—and then he inexplicably fell over dead. The dramatic news resulted in great curiosity, and large numbers of prisoners came to hear the message of the green pastures. Many became Christians; as they were released from prison one by one, they went forth preaching the Gospel.

One of these, Serguey Basarov, became an effective evangelist and pastor in the city of Isafara in northern Tajikistan. Because of his faithful witness, Islamists fired sixteen rounds into his room as he was engaged in his devotions, striking him in the hand, leg, and heart. But nothing stopped the progress of the Gospel. According to the Baptist Union of Tajikistan, over 75 percent of their church-planters are former prisoners who found the Good Shepherd and His green pastures while in prison.

Wherever you are and whatever your need, the same Shepherd is seeking to find, love, guard, guide, and bless you. The Twenty-third Psalm isn't just a beautiful narration; it's a living reality for those acquainted with its divine author.

Years ago in college, I came across a story I've never forgotten. At a social gathering in London an actor was asked to give a recitation. He quoted Psalm Twenty-three with pauses, inflections, and remarkable timbre of voice. A murmur of admiration ran through the crowd.

An aged minister then rose to recite the same passage. When he finished, all eyes were filled with tears. Later the actor approached the minister and said, "Do you know the difference between my recitation and yours? I know the psalm, but you know the Shepherd."

May God help us know both! And then you can say with me come what may:

The Lord is my Shepherd—That's Enough!

Acknowledgments

$\mathcal{I}$ want to express my deepest thanks to:

The Donelson Fellowship in Nashville, where I presented this material in sermonic form.

Chris Ferebee, who believed in this project and launched it.

Sealy Yates of Yates and Yates, whose sage and seasoned advice is invaluable to me.

My assistant, Sherry Anderson, who multitasks with the best of them.

My creative team at Clearly Media, including Joshua Rowe, Stephen Fox, and Michael Walker, whose marketing and social networking expertise are any writer's best friend.

My publisher and coffee buddy, Jonathan Merkh, a dear friend for more than thirty years.

My senior editor, Philis Boultinghouse, whose confidence and competence have made this book a joy to write.

My developmental editor, Nicci Jordan Hubert, whose keen eye and sense of unity and pacing greatly strengthened this book.

All those who have shared their stories about sheep or the Twenty-third Psalm with me and allowed me to use them.

My three girls, Victoria, Hannah, and Grace, whose shepherding instincts have taught me much about life.

My dear wife, Katrina, who reviews every word I write and corrects many of them.

And you, dear friend, for reading this book and recommending it to others. God bless you!

Notes

Prologue

1. William Evans, *The Shepherd Psalm* (Chicago: The Bible Institute Colportage Association, 1921), 7.
2. Frederick B. Meyer, *The Shepherd Psalm* (New Canaan, CT: Keats Publishing, Inc., 1984), 13.
3. Shared personally with the author and used with permission.
4. Originally appeared in the periodical *The Gospel Herald*. Reprinted by Paul Lee Tan in *Encyclopedia of 7700 Illustrations* (Rockville, MD: Assurance Publishers, 1980), 498.

Introduction

1. Based on a personal interview with Maurice Pink on Sunday, January 1, 2012, and used with permission.
2. John Stevenson, *The Lord Our Shepherd: An Exposition of the Twenty-third Psalm* (New York: Robert Carter, 1845), v, vi.
3. Ibid., vi.

Chapter 1

1. Robert C. McQuilkin, *The Lord Is My Shepherd* (Columbia, SC: Columbia Bible College, 1938), 5.
2. Paula Simmons and Carol Ekarius, *Storey's Guide to Raising Sheep* (North Adams, MA: Storey Publishing, 2009), 13.

3. Roy Gustafson, *In His Land Seeing Is Believing* (Minneapolis, MN: World Wide Publications, 1980), 42.

4. Ibid., 49–50.

5. To prevent readers from speaking this name, scribes took steps to create textual markers to remind readers not to use this name in reading aloud. They used the vowels from the word *Adonai* and placed them with the consonants YHWH to remind readers to say "Adonai" instead of "YHWH." In this way, the scribes maintained both reverence and scriptural accuracy when the divine name was used. The German theologians gave it as a "J" sound at the beginning, a "V" sound in the middle, and they transliterated the text markers (the vowel sounds from Adonai), and that's why some translations say Jehovah. But as far as we can determine, the best pronunciation is something like "Yahweh."

6. Widely reported, including in the *London Daily Mail,* "'I Can't Be Sure God Does Not Exist': World's Most Notorious Atheist Richard Dawkins Admits He Is in Fact Agnostic," February 24, 2012, at www.dailymail.co.uk, accessed March 12, 2012.

7. The italicized emphasis on the word *is* in these verses is mine.

Chapter 2

1. McQuilkin, *The Lord Is My Shepherd,* 9.

2. This old story appears in many places, including J. Wilber Chapman, *The Secret of a Happy Day* (Grand Rapids, MI: Baker Book House, reprint of 1899 edition), 24–25, and in H. Edwin Young, *The Lord Is . . .* (Nashville: Broadman Press, 1981), 17–19.

3. Evans, *The Shepherd Psalm,* 9.

4. Tommy Walker, "He Knows My Name," at www.tommywalker.net.

5. Charles Haddon Spurgeon from his sermon "The Sheep and Their Shepherd."

6. Excerpt from the poem "The Ninety and Nine," by Elizabeth C. Clephane, 1868.

7. John Muir, *The Writings of John Muir,* vol. 2 (Boston: Houghton Mifflin Company, 1916), 129.

8. Quoted by Virginia Paul, *This Was Sheep Ranching Yesterday and Today* (Seattle: Superior Publishing Company, n.d.), 55.

9. Ibid., 83.

Chapter 3

1. McQuilkin, *The Lord Is My Shepherd*, 11.
2. Allan C. Emery, *A Turtle on a Fencepost* (Waco, TX: Word Books, 1979), 53.
3. From a clipping in my files. Source unknown.
4. *Congressional Record*: House, September 29, 1998, p. 22652.

Chapter 4

1. McQuilkin, *The Lord Is My Shepherd*, 38.
2. Paul, *This Was Sheep Ranching Yesterday and Today*, 45.
3. Diamondfield Jack escaped the gallows only to be struck and killed by a taxicab in Las Vegas in 1949.
4. Hunt Janin, *Fort Bridger, Wyoming* (Jefferson, NC: McFarland & Co., 2001), 123.
5. Paul, *This Was Sheep Ranching Yesterday and Today*, 49.
6. Simmons and Ekarius, *Storey's Guide to Raising Sheep*, 99.
7. Jane Rumph and C. Peter Wagner, *Stories from the Front Lines: Power Evangelism in Today's World* (Grand Rapids, MI: Chosen 1996; Fairfax, VA: Xulon, 2001), 135–139.
8. Told to me personally and used with permission.
9. Personally related to me and used with permission. For similar stories, see my book *Angels: True Stories* (Nashville: Thomas Nelson, 2011).
10. Martha A. Cook, "The Lord Will Provide," 1870.
11. Newell Dwight Hillis and William Henry Channing, *Right Living as a Fine Art* (New York: Fleming H. Revell Company, 1899), 8.
12. Evans, *The Shepherd Psalm*, 27.
13. Based on a personal interview with Edith Pouquette and on the article, "Centennial Celebration: Four Generations of Pouquettes Operated the Red Hill Sheep Company," in *The Williams–Grand Canyon News*, February 12, 2012, www.williamsnews.com, accessed March 13, 2012.
14. Evans, *The Shepherd Psalm*, 27–28.

Chapter 5

1. McQuilkin, *The Lord Is My Shepherd*, 14.
2. Based on email correspondence with Earl Langly in 2011, and used with permission.
3. Phillip Keller, *A Shepherd Looks at Psalm 23* (Grand Rapids, MI: Zondervan, 1970), 59–62.

4. Corrie ten Boom, *Tramp for the Lord* (Fort Washington, PA: CLC Publications, 1974), 116.

5. Henry Varley, *Terse Talk on Timely Topics* (London: James Nisbet & Co., 1884), 151–152.

6. Henry Martyn, *Journal and Letters of the Rev. Henry Martyn,* vol. 1 (London: R. B. Seeley and W. Burnside, 1837), 227.

Chapter 6

1. McQuilkin, *The Lord Is My Shepherd,* 14.

2. Based on a personal interview with Edith Pouquette and used with permission.

3. Paul, *This Was Sheep Ranching Yesterday and Today,* 45.

4. D. L. Salsbury in "The Shepherd's Lament," quoted in Simmons and Ekarius, *Storey's Guide to Raising Sheep,* vi.

5. J. I. Packer, *God's Plans for You* (Wheaton, IL: Crossway Books, 2001), 98.

6. Anees T. Baroody, *The Syrian Shepherd* (Chicago: published privately, 1916), 13.

7. Ibid., 46–47.

8. C. H. Mackintosh, *Notes on Exodus* (New York: Loizeaux Brothers, Inc., 1880), 15–16.

9. Adoniram Judson Gordon, *The Holy Spirit in Missions* (New York: Fleming H. Revell Company, 1893), 94–95.

10. F. B. Meyer, *Steps into the Blessed Life* (Philadelphia: Henry Altemus Company, 1896), 36–37.

11. Fanny Crosby, "All the Way My Savior Leads Me" in *Brightest and Best* (New York: Biglow & Main, 1875), number 65.

Chapter 7

1. McQuilkin, *The Lord Is My Shepherd,* 16–17.

2. Based on a personal interview on March 19, 2012, and used with permission.

3. Martin Luther King Jr., "I've Been to the Mountaintop," delivered April 3, 1968, Memphis, Tennessee.

4. Charles L. Allen, *God's Psychiatry* (New York: Fleming Revell Co., 1952), 25–26.

5. Timothy East, *Death Bed Scenes: or, The Christian's Companion on Entering the Dark Valley* (London: Francis Westley, 1825), 121–131.

6. Charles Haddon Spurgeon in his sermon "Jacob's Waking Exclamation" from July 21, 1861. I have taken the liberty of condensing and updating some of Spurgeon's archaic language for this quote.

Chapter 8

1. McQuilkin, *The Lord Is My Shepherd*, 17.
2. Alexandra Zayas, "World War II Veteran, Former POW, Takes Freedom as It Comes," *Tampa Bay Times*, November 10, 2011; available online at http://www.tampabay.com/news/humaninterest/world-war-ii-veteran-former-pow-takes-freedom-as-it-comes/*1201076*.

Chapter 9

1. McQuilkin, *The Lord Is My Shepherd*, 18–19.
2. Based on a personal interview on March 1, 2012, and used with permission.
3. Jill Briscoe, *A Little Pot of Oil* (Sisters, OR: Multnomah Publishers, 2003), ch. 1, quote on p. 22.
4. Billy Graham, *Just as I Am* (HarperSanFrancisco/Zondervan, 1997), 212.
5. Frances R. Havergal in her hymn "Lord, Speak to Me," 1872.
6. Hannah W. Smith and M. E. Dieter, *The Christian's Secret of a Holy Life* (Oak Harbor, WA: Logos Research Systems, Inc., YEAR?), entry for February 13.
7. Charles F. Deems in his hymn "I Shall Not Want," 1872.

Chapter 10

1. McQuilkin, *The Lord Is My Shepherd*, 19.
2. Andrew Lang and Henry Justice Ford, *The Red Book of Animal Stories* (London: Longmans, Green, & Co., 1899), 268–269.
3. Simmons and Ekarius, *Storey's Guide to Raising Sheep*, 135.
4. These terms and their variations are widely reproduced. Part of my list comes from Simmons and Ekarius, *Storey's Guide to Raising Sheep*, 144.
5. Paul, *This Was Sheep Ranching Yesterday and Today*, 86.
6. McQuilkin, *The Lord Is My Shepherd*, 35.
7. Robert J. Morgan, *My All in All* (Nashville: B&H Publishing Group, 2008), 2–3. This book of daily devotions is now published under the title *All to Jesus*.

Chapter 11

1. McQuilkin, *The Lord Is My Shepherd* , 15.

Conclusion

1. Allen, *God's Psychiatry*, 13–14.

Additional resources are available at
www.robertjmorgan.com

The Lord Is My Shepherd Study Guide
A Group Study Guide and Leader's Handbook
for this book

Twenty-three Trails
A Free Personal Set of Devotional Bible Studies
Based on Psalm 23

The 23rd Psalm
The Lord Is My Shepherd—That's Enough
An attractive sixteen-page digest of this book
priced for mass distribution by churches
and individuals

Book Robert J. Morgan for your next corporate event,
church gathering, or special service.
Visit robertjmorgan.com/speaking
for a speaker's kit and for inquiries.